Learning to Use What You ALREADY KNOW

Learning to Use What You ALREADY KNOW

Stephen A. Stumpf & Joel R. De Luca

Illustrated by Dan Shefelman

Berrett-Koehler Publishers
San Francisco

Berrett-Koehler Publishers, Inc.
155 Montgomery St.
San Francisco, CA 94104-4109
Tel: 415-288-0260   Fax: 415-362-2512

Ordering Information
Individual sales. Berrett-Koehler publications are available through most bookstores. They can also be ordered direct from Berrett-Koehler at the address above.

Quantity sales. Special discounts are available on quantity purchases by corporations, associations, and others. For details, contact the "Special Sales Department" at the Berrett-Koehler address above.

Orders for college textbook/course adoption use. Please contact Berrett-Koehler Publishers at the address above.

Orders by U.S. trade bookstores and wholesalers. Please contact Publishers Group West, 4065 Hollis St., P.O. Box 8843, Emeryville, CA 94662; 510-658-3453; 1-800-788-3123.

Printed in the United States of America

Printed on acid-free and recycled paper that meets the strictest state and U.S. guidelines for recycled paper (50 percent recycled waste, including 10 percent postconsumer waste).

Library of Congress Cataloging-in-Publication Data

Stumpf, Stephen A.
    Learning to use what you already know / Stephen A. Stumpf and Joel R. DeLuca : illustrated by Dan Shefelman.
        p.   cm.
    Includes bibliographical references and index.
    ISBN 1-881052-55-9
    1. Creativity in business. 2. Insight. 3. Problem solving.
I. DeLuca, Joel R., 1948–   . II. Shefelman, Dan. III. Title.
HD53.S78   1994   94–16997
650. 1—dc20   CIP

First Edition
99 98 97 96 95 94   10 9 8 7 6 5 4 3 2 1

Book Design & Production: Pacific West Publishing Service

In great appreciation of the "everyday" people who have contributed to and nurtured our development of insights. You are heroes for the next generation.

FRAMES
CONTENTS

SETTING
P R E F A C E

"YOU KNOW MORE THAN YOU KNOW!" An absurd statement until it is clarified – which is our purpose in writing this book.

What we mean by such a statement is that the total you, which includes more than your conscious thought, contains resources that can yield practical skills and wisdom. For example, what part of you knows how to ride a bicycle – probably not the conscious part. Have you ever tried to explain the mechanics of riding a bike to someone? Or, what part of you wakes you up two minutes before the alarm goes off?

Learning to Use What You Already Know is about insights. We use the word insight to mean *looking inward to make connections among previously unrelated ideas, people, events, or situations – and creating new meaning out of those connections.*

You may wonder: "How is a book of other peoples' insights going to be of use to me?" We are the first generation to truly experience an information explosion while having personalized computer technology to cope with it; yet most of us have not made the connections among the bits of knowledge and experience we have accumulated that will lead to crystallization of our insights. We have not taken the time to reflect on our experiences in a systematic way so as to precipitate lasting insights.

Learning to Use What You Already Know is a guide for increasing our effectiveness as we grapple with work life. It will stimulate your thinking about the experiences that you are having. Some of our insights will be your insights. Reading them will yield a quick "ah ha" reaction, and the thought that "I knew that!"

Other times our insight will stimulate an "in other words" reaction. You will be having a similar insight, but you would describe it *"in other words."* We try to stimulate these "in other words" ideas through illustrations and questions at the end of each frame (chapter). Once an insight occurs, you might want to mentally record it to be replayed and used by you. Better yet, record it in the book as you go. Feel free to enhance the graphics, make notes in the columns, or write new captions for the illustrations.

Reading *Learning to Use What You Already Know* is a serious and fun experience. What is more serious than a child at play? We invite you to seriously play with our, and *your,* insights. Developing insights is like doing a "connect-the-dots" picture. As the dots are connected, a figure emerges, only the dots to be connected in your development of insights are not numbered.

HOW TO USE THIS BOOK
TO MAXIMIZE YOUR EFFECTIVENESS

As you play with *Learning to Use What You Already Know* we encourage you to connect the dots, to develop some maps of personal insights. You might think of these dot maps as frames in your motion picture of life. In fact, we tend to think of the chapters in this book as frames. Read the chapters in any order. Go with your interests and energy. While there are some linkages among the insights addressed in different frames, this should pose no problem. It may stimulate you to read a frame previously skipped over, or it may lead to a distinct personal insight.

If you are reading this book on your own, have a pen and paper near by. The notes that you make as you go are an excellent index to your emerging insights. Do not be discouraged if you cannot immediately answer all of the questions at the end of each section. Sometimes an "ah ha" comes hours, even days afterwards as your experience fills in some new dots of which you were previously unaware.

It can be quite stimulating to read the book with your partner or some colleagues or coworkers. It is fun to bounce ideas back and forth. It is also possible for people who know your working style to offer you feedback on your approach to things; they can point out both positive and negative behaviors that you may not have noticed yourself.

If you are focusing your developmental efforts on a particular area (e.g., managing change, improving interpersonal relationships, developing creativity), let the index be your guide. We have tried to identify the interrelationships among sections in the index.

Redoing some of the exercises, or answering some of the questions after a few weeks or some significant life event, can be very fruitful. It is often the case that after we are shaken up by something, we are more open to reflecting and connecting the dots to develop new insights.

We feel confident that the insights discussed in this book will be a useful guide to your thinking. They are likely to parallel your insights or stimulate new ones. As you discover them, we invite you to share with us a favorite insight for a future volume of *Learning to Use What You Already Know* — in words, pictures, photographs, or whatever means communicates the insight clearly. Before using this insight, we will contact you for written permission and form of acknowledgement. (Be sure to give us your name, address, and phone number with any insights you share.)

ACKNOWLEDGEMENTS

The ideas and insights that we share have come to us over time from many places. The writings of other authors have often stimulated our insights. Sometimes an insight is routed in an event we experienced; other times it crystallizes out of a vicarious experience such as watching television, listening to the radio, or observing others (particularly children!). On occasion, an insight is the result of analytic thinking – being rational, logical.

There are many people who have influenced our thinking: a special thanks to Eugene Arnone, Zenas Block, Roger Dunbar, Michael Kitson, Bob McDowell, Kathy Morris, Thomas Mullen, Richard Stumpf, and Dale Zand. Others have influenced us through our interactions and business activities with them, including Susan Berger, Sabra Brock, Anne Hayden, Douglas Hofstadter, David Kreischer, Robert Longman, Lorna Simon, Candace Ulrich, and Karen Watson.

Others who have contributed to this book are part of a team, the Management Simulation Projects Group at New York University: Catherine Ahern, Maria Arnone, Deborah Barrows, Hrach Bedrosian, Richard Green, Susan Heinbuch, Mary McBride, Sidney Nachman, and Monica Shay.

No book makes it to print without the extensive help of an editor, reviewers, and lots of supporting cast. We are thankful for the assistance of Patricia Anderson, Deane Gradous, Chuck Kormanski, Andrea Markowitz, Sue McKibbin, Steven Piersanti, Elizabeth Swenson, Alan Trist, and John Willig.

We particularly appreciate the support of our families and friends who both encouraged us and put up with us over the years. We thank you.

Stephen A. Stumpf, Tampa, Florida
Joel R. DeLuca, Philadelphia, Pensylvania
Dam Shefelman, New York, New York
May, 1994

Introduction

THE POWER OF INSIGHT AT WORK

INSIGHTS are about connecting the fragmented knowledge in different parts of ourselves into a more integrated whole so that we can act in concert with our intentions. Insights occur when two previously unconnected parts connect and a flash of understanding is experienced. This is the result of new, enriched neural connections being made. The sound of an insight may take the form of an "ah ha," "eureka!" "BFO" (blinding flash of the obvious), or a quiet "hmmm." Or it may appear as a big smile, or leaning back in a chair with an expression of contentment, or standing up to express enthusiasm and excitement. Insights bring enjoyment and build the mind's capacity to interact more effectively with the environment. This suggests that:

- Insights are personal. While you (and we) can share an insight, the insight will have a unique meaning for each of us.

- Insights are rigorous connections we make among disparate thoughts – these connections seem to apply to many situations.

- Insights are clarifications of previously confusing or ambiguous thoughts.

- Insights are useful understandings of complex situations.

- Insights come from the knowledge we have acquired in conjunction with the things we have experienced (either personally or vicariously). The more education, wisdom, and experiences one has, the more potential to develop insights. The raw material for insights is available to everyone, but in differing quantities and forms. Whether or not it is used to develop insights is an open question.

• Insights are developed through reflecting on current experiences in light of previous experiences. It is the reflective process that permits insights to crystallize. Without reflection, learning is limited to current understandings and thoughts without the benefit of feedback.

The brain is a natural learning system. It loves to learn. Recent advances in neuroscience have shown that the brain is a system made up of many subsystems. Some subsystems have knowledge not contained in others. This is attributed to the fact that the brain evolved over aeons in a rather haphazard way where one part of the brain evolved on top of older parts. The reptilian brain evolved first and is the home of our "fight-flight" survival response. Then the mammalian brain, home of our emotions, evolved on top of our reptilian brain. Next the cortex, home of our intellect and rational thought, evolved. Each of these subsystem brains have their own agendas and at times these agendas do not coincide. This is why we make "mistakes" which at the time seemed logical and appropriate actions. We later admit, "I'm only human" in response to such mistakes.

Insights are the building blocks that our natural learning system uses to guide our behavior. Once an insight has been linked to experience, learning has occurred and one increases his capacity to act in new ways. Consider the following:

When did you have your last insight into a problem, person, or situation? If you cannot recall what the insight was, can you remember the feeling you had as the insight became apparent? It felt good, didn't it? For a few moments you felt particularly aware, sensitive, perceptive, and maybe even empowered, clever, and shrewd. We all need these feelings to cope effectively with a complex and changing world that, all too often, seems to defy analysis and logical thinking.

Inspiration for your insights is simple: You have experienced many intensive work periods and have come to personal understandings of work, life, and social relationships through the process. Ask yourself, "What insights have I developed from my recent activities, accomplishments, and frustrations? Several may come to mind. We hope to stimulate your thinking about your insights by sharing some of ours.

The organization of this book mirrors the *insight-to-learning* process. Each chapter (which we think of as a *frame* in a movie reel) starts with an *insight,* provides a *context (story)* for reflection, summarizes the context with a *lesson statement* to represent key learnings, and concludes with *questions* to stimulate your insights.

Since insights are simplifications of complex phenomena, they can be articulated in short statements. We share our insights in the frame titles. The insight is then clarified through stories that reflect our past experiences and knowledge. By embedding the insight in an example, a richer context for your insight development is provided. We do this in a variety of ways, depending on the nature of the insight and how we first connected the dots ourselves. We may ground or anchor an insight by providing short examples or anecdotes, by describing a detailed situation, by proposing an analogy, or by positioning the insight within a conceptual framework. Illustrations are used to make a visual representation of a context, or to present an insight "in other words". We have created some "marginal characters" to add a sense of texture and character to the insights. Insights do not always first emerge as words – they may begin with images, visualizations, emotions, or abstractions. We have tried to share our insights, and stimulate your's through variety in the media of presentation.

We include a *lesson statement* in each frame to reinforce and remind us of the insight's key message. Your insights, and ability to develop insights, will be enhanced by following a process such as: state your insight, describe it, ground it in your knowledge and experience (through a reflective process whereby you find examples that support the insight's main premise), and finally create a summary statement of the lesson learned. We conclude each frame with *questions* to begin this insight-to-learning process.

The organization of the frames may at first seem chaotic. In a way, this arrangement is an application of chaos theory – order is not immediately apparent but it may still exist. Insights are neither predictable nor orderly. As suggested by chaos theory, there may be an underlying order that can be perceived over time. What themes emerge for you?

1 Life Repeats Itself Until We Learn

A PERSON we know has difficulty getting up for work each morning. It is not that he dislikes work – quite the contrary – and it is not that he likes the tension associated with rushing, or being late to work, or listening to his partner complain that he will be late. But nothing changes, no matter what he feels in the morning nor what his partner says. Life will repeat itself until he learns. Learns what? That is hard for someone else to say. Maybe he has to learn that if he goes to bed earlier, he will wake up more easily. Maybe it is that he has to shorten his morning shower to 10 minutes, or his dawdling time to 5 minutes, or set his alarm earlier. But what one *can* say is that he will continue this uncomfortable pattern until he learns how to stop it.

What is learning? Is it education? Instruction? Study? Schooling? Memorization? Each of these activities is intended to facilitate learning. *But they are not learning.* Learning, we have come to realize, is the acquired knowledge and skill that we retain − consciously and unconsciously − that changes our behaviors. If we do not or cannot do things differently as a result of our education and study, then what is it that we learned? We may know more (sometimes called knowledge acquisition). We may feel differently (sometimes called emotional awareness). But without practice, without actually doing something, have we actually learned?

Much of what is taught is intended to provide us with knowledge − facts and information that are believed to be true by the teachers, scientists, and historians at the time it is conveyed. This information may have been experienced by us as "great stuff" or "boring stuff." Our response to it probably depends on our interests and the educational setting and instructor at the time. If you are like us, whenever "learning" took the form of memorization for the sake of testing well on exams, it was unpleasant, boring, and induced negative stress. In hindsight, it was not learning at all since little of it is used or remembered today. In reflecting on your own education, instruction, schooling, or study, has it been more ritual than learning? How much of your formal education do you remember and use?

While you are meeting us as authors, we have had other "occupations." Joel was a physicist; Steve was a chemical engineer. Collectively we have 10 years of college and graduate work in the hard sciences. What we remember is a way of scientific thinking, a few scientific facts (some of which we sometimes discover are no longer accurate), and about 50 bits of jargon that seem to transcend the textbooks in which we first came across them and now seem to apply to everyday activities.

As educators and consultants, we have many opportunities to inquire about the learning of others. Of the several thousand people with whom we have discussed the topic of learning, most estimate that they are able to recall about half of what was conveyed in primary school, a quarter of what was provided in secondary school, and little of what was acquired in college and graduate school a year or two after completion. (A disappointing finding for us college professors.) Should not these percentages be reversed, with more learning taking place in college? Probably not. Learning is often cumulative; we would not be able to read the secondary school texts if we did not learn how to read and develop a strong vocabulary in primary school. Nor would college calculus be accessible if algebra was not learned in high school.

Educational systems often provide information in a ritualistic manner because the sharing and acquisition of knowledge is easier to orchestrate and evaluate collectively than are experiences and activities that stimulate individual learning. For many of us, educational systems have emphasized memorization. Memorization of facts is important to our functioning in society, but it is hard work. When education becomes hard work, we stop having fun and begin to think of education as a separate part of life. We unlearn what we had learned as a child – that every day is full of learning opportunities that can be exciting and energizing. We begin to treat education as work – something to be constrained to specific parts of the day and to be left behind when we go home.

Fortunately, life is wiser than we may be during most of our formal education. When life wants us to learn something, it demands that we do things differently. If we do not, life repeats the lesson until we do. Life provides us with lessons very persistently.

Some may interpret our view regarding learning to mean that all of life's experiences are instructional events. By collecting as many experiences as possible, you become well educated. Not necessarily so.

Until one connects the experiences and finds the patterns among them, or places the experiences into contexts additional to those in which the experiences occurred, learning is not likely to take place. Our role in learning is much more active than memorizing facts and collecting experiences. We continually decide which experiences to seek, what questions to ask, which situations to explore, and then attempt to answer "What does it mean to me."

You may ask, "Why is it that education doesn't also help people connect their experiences to achieve much deeper learning?" We are not sure. Formal education *could* help people to develop their insights. But, this does not seem to be what most formal educators or their educational systems want to do. Educational systems from grade five through post baccalaureate work seem more focused on conveying facts and knowledge linked to specific disciplines than personal insight development.

This was our experience. Was it yours?

> *We may learn from life, but we are our own teacher. Life is not the teacher – it is the lessons.*

1. Reflect on a recent interaction with a colleague, spouse, or child. What occurred in this interaction that is a "repeat" of many previous interactions?

   (If you have thought of something negative, push yourself to also think of something positive, and vice versa.) Note the "repeat" behaviors below.

 Repeated Positives:

 Repeated Negatives:

2. What are the lessons that these repeat behaviors might be trying to convey?

3. What can you discover from the patterns in the interaction? What can you change in these patterns?

2 Go with Your FLOW For Optimal Experiences

REFLECT for a minute on the best experiences in your life. When did they occur? What were you doing? What did it feel like? The best moments in our lives have been when we are totally engrossed in something physically or mentally that is personally meaningful and challenging. It can occur while trying to resolve a business issue, revise a book chapter, or swimming an 800-meter race. We see it in others when they are tackling something which is exciting for them.

Mihaly Csikszentmihalyi's book *FLOW: The Psychology of Optimal Experience* defines such moments as *flow*. His research found that you generally reach flow when:

- you are confronting tasks that you have a chance of completing;

- you are able to concentrate on what you are doing;

- the task has clear goals;

- the task provides immediate feedback;

- you act with deep but effortless involvement that removes from awareness other aspects of your life; and

- you experience a sense of control over the activities.

Two immediate effects of flow are that your concern for self disappears during the process, only to emerge afterward even stronger; and your sense of time is altered – sometimes greatly shortened, sometimes lengthened.

The longest period of flow that Steve can remember lasted about 8 hours – on one physics problem (and he was a chemical engineering major!). As Steve recalls, "I never did get the textbook answer to that problem, but I probably learned most of the semester of physics that evening. I became totally engaged in various scenarios and thought processes to resolve a complex problem. It felt good to work hard, to stretch my own limits in a voluntary effort to accomplish something. I was *not* cramming for an exam. In fact, I have some difficulty reaching flow when I study for tests because my anxiety distracts me. I do not believe that you can be made to experience flow; yet, you can let it happen."

Flow is productive and enjoyable. The deep reward we give ourselves during and after flow is a prime motivator for future activity. Reaching flow may be effortless – such as becoming engrossed in a new computer game, or it may involve substantial effort in such tasks as mastering a tough musical score, making a gourmet meal for friends, or running a marathon. Larry Bird, and other master athletes, often discuss their best games as flow experiences. They performed to their ideal with less struggle than anticipated.

Everyone has flow experiences, but not everyone is aware of having them. Nor do we actively seek flow as often as we might. All too often, flow is something that just happens – often to be interrupted by someone or something unaware of the happiness that we are experiencing. Yet, by understanding the concept of flow, and by creating conditions conducive to flow, we may be able to spend more time in the flow state rather than waiting for it to occur.

**Recognizing your personal flow
experiences, then embracing and
building the flow process, contributes
greatly to personal fulfillment.**

---

1. I tend to experience a flow-like experience when
    I (circle all that apply):

    jog, swim, ride a bike, or walk for exercise
    fish, hunt, or ride a horse for sport
    read a good book
    write a letter to a friend

    get into a technical problem
    play sports; which ones? . . . .
     watch sports; which ones?. . . . .

    play a musical instrument

    talk to . . . .
    clean the . . . .
    do the . . . .
    listen to . . . .

2. When do you experience flow at work? List the kinds of things that lead to flow experiences.

3. What can you do to achieve flow at work more often?

4. When might flow be detrimental to a work situation?

3   Follow Your Energy

P EOPLE have energy for some activities and not others. You would think it is obvious to them where their energy lies. But it rarely is. We need to become an observer of our own behavior to determine where our inner forces are directing us.

Ask yourself where your energy lies. When the pressure is off, what stimulates you? What are your "natural highs." Where does the excitement come from? What is the source of your energy and what do you do with it? One person we know gains energy from music, jazz in particular. She can listen to it intensely, blocking out other stimuli entirely. After listening to an album or visiting a jazz club, she is energized for other things – like cold calling a prospective client to see if she can arrange a meeting.

Another friend gets his energy from movies – not television. There must be something about the movie theater, the big screen, and the intensity of the presentation that goes beyond the story. He can watch an afternoon movie then return to the office for four hours of quality work.

Energy comes from a driving force within you. Your driving force moves you from passive curiosity to active exploration and exertion. *What moves you from one state to the next?* It may be a single motivator, or a few motivators, but few people have more than a handful of driving forces. Your driving force is more likely to be an instinctive or intuitive response than a learned or planned one. Birds flock to warmer climates in the winter. They must have an inner energy for this trip that keeps them going. Marathon runners, deal makers in investment banking, musicians, and many others find the energy to keep going.

The value in identifying our energy sources is not for the good times. When things are going well, we probably have more energy than we can effectively use. We need to know our driving forces for the slow times; for the times that we feel troubled. By hooking into our driving force at these times, we are able to continue, and sometimes even prosper. Marsha Sinetan's book, *Do What You Love, The Money Will Follow*, captures this point well.

Over the course of several seminars, we asked several hundred people to identify where their energy comes from. Six out of ten had difficulty doing this until after they have taken some time to *actively* reflect on their lives. If your driving force is not immediately apparent, do the following: keep a diary of what you do and how you feel about it for three days, one of which is a weekend day. At the beginning of each hour, log the events that lasted more than a couple of minutes the previous hour in the diary. Using this information, ask yourself, "Why did I do these things?" and "Which activities were under my control?" "Which were uplifting and energizing?"

This creates an information base on which your intuition will work. By looking for patterns in activities and motives, you will be able to identify your driving forces – those forces which provide the energy to do more. Go with your energy as often as the environment will allow.

---

*Following our natural energy allows
us to accomplish more of the things
that we value, enjoy the process
more, and deplete our energy
resources the least.*

---

1. While driving forces vary from person to person,
   some of the most common ones are:

   - The desire to excel in all that I do.
   - The desire to excel in one particular activity.
   - Wanting to be with people.
   - Wanting to participate in some event.
   - Wanting to help people.
   - Wanting to master a specific field.
   - Wanting to avoid failure or rejection.
   - Being accepted by others.
   - Being appreciated by others.
   - Attaining self-sufficiency.
   - Becoming wealthy.
   - Using a particular skill.
   - Being "free" or independent.
   - Creating personal time to reflect.
   - Wanting to share ideas and spirituality.

   Is your driving force listed above? If not, what
   are your sources of energy?

2. Work becomes play when I am . . . . . .

3. I have the most energy for doing . . . .
   . . . . .while at work.

4. Type your driving forces on a card and put it
   where it can serve as a reminder:

   FOLLOW YOUR ENERGY!

4 Lack of Fit Is Not Failure

WITH SO many different tasks to do and areas within which to work, no one should by nature become a personal failure. We all have limitations. But limitations are not necessarily deficiencies to be corrected. Everyone has many distinct interests, skills, and abilities. Everyone has talents. *What seems to be rare is the willingness to follow one's talents to the unknown places they might lead.* It must be easier to put ourselves down for what we cannot do – our deficiencies – than it is to find or construct ways to apply the talents that we have. If the ugly duckling tried to fix itself based on "peer" feedback, it would never have discovered it was a swan!

To overcome this personal put-down, a career counseling industry has been created. Its primary function is to assist people with different aptitudes to take the journey to different positions which require their distinctive skills. It is a task of finding a comfortable match between the person's talents and the job's requirements.

Since both people and tasks change, obtaining fit is not something to be done only once in a lifetime. Matching skills and interests to tasks is an ongoing process. Sometimes the fit is particularly strong. Other times, it is not. But the goal remains the same – seek and accept tasks and positions that leverage our strengths first, and support the development of areas that we want to enhance second.

With so much self-help and personal growth counseling available today, we are hesitant to down-play the seeking of personal development tasks. Yet, what works best for you? Is it easier and more productive to leverage your strengths, do what comes naturally rather than to focus on your limitations? The fear that creeps into the "go with your strengths" philosophy is "What if no one values my skills, what will I do then?" This fear lures us to develop extra skills rather than find more ways and places to use the skills that we already enjoy. Tina Turner is a talented blues singer – a skill that she began to develop through gospel singing as a youth. She learned how to use an existing talent in new ways for different audiences. Similarly, Joel's study of physics has served him well in analyzing the forces and counter-forces of organizational change efforts and in being an organizational development practitioner. He learned to use an existing talent in new ways as well.

A manager at the American Express Company shared her experience and insight:

"I've had two bosses in the last year, each of whom often criticized me on a task that was part of my job that I didn't do as well as they wanted – real nitty-gritty stuff that requires remembering jargon and details. I decided to look for a course or colleague to help me learn and retain the detail, then an insight hit. 'Why am I doing this? I don't like this stuff to begin with, and if I get good at it, they will give me more of it.'

"I decided to locate the colleague – not to learn from him, but to share the task with him. This colleague has now assumed responsibility for the task and it is being done well. My boss is happy, I'm happy. And the colleague that has taken the responsibility for that other task is delighted that his skills are valued and being seen by more people."

Seeking fit is not meant to imply that we should never perform a task for which we have little or unknown aptitude. Trying new things is how we often determine our aptitudes. It is through our successes and mistakes that we learn what it is that we do well. Successes keep our egos alive. Mistakes help to keep our learning alive; mistakes can be the beginning of a discovery process. Repeated mistakes without learning or changing tasks may lead to failure. And, failure can be a debilitating human experience. It will drain your energy and curtail your interests.

---

*Those that do not learn from their
mistakes are frustrated; the rest of us
are on journeys to positions that fit
our interests, values, and aptitudes.*

---

1. The last checkpoint that I passed on my journey
to positions that better fit my interests, values,
and aptitudes was. . .

2. The skills that I used to reach this goal were. . .

3. What is happening at work this week that is
calling for the application of my skills? Where
can I contribute?

5 If You Get It Right the First Time, Every Time, You Aren't Risking Enough

TOTAL quality is the challenge of the 90's. Continuous quality improvement is sought, with fewer mistakes along the way. The challenge was "zero defects" in the 60's, "efficiency" in the 70's, and "efficiency and effectiveness" in the 80's. So businesses have been very concerned with doing things "right." But how does doing things right affect personal growth, learning, and the betterment of our world?

Total quality is an appropriate battle cry for organizations whose primary goals are market share and profits. It seems less appropriate as a general battle cry for the processes of human development and discovery. Some people become uncomfortable when they hear "total quality." To them it seems to imply finding the best way to do something and then doing it that way, possibly forever.

If it is not seeking total quality, what is it that is exhilarating about personal growth and life-long learning? We think it is discovery, exploration, and trying new things. It is coming to understand -- intellectually and emotionally -- more of life. These outcomes involve some degree of trial and error, and the obvious reality that all will not be done perfectly each time. The risk of making a mistake cannot be avoided if something new is to be experienced.

In most activities where performance is assessed relative to objective measures of past performances – such as running, swimming, high jumping, or the units of output from a production activity – the real leaps forward in performance are due to changes in the ways things are traditionally done. Such changes did not just appear. Someone, often many people, began risking something and learning from their mistakes. This leads to more exploring, more risk-taking, and more discoveries of what does not work.

For a few, the quest leads to an alternative way of performing that works better for them than the more traditional way. No one even considered doing a high jump such that your back would go over the bar first. If you are running forward, your front should logically go over a high bar first. It was ridiculous to think that high jumpers should somehow rotate on an imaginary axis going through them from head to toe such that their back would face the high bar at the peak of their jump – until it became *the* way to high jump as ever new high jumping records were set.

But, how much should we risk? Risk involves overcoming fears – which is more easily said than done. How do we know how much risk to take relative to the possible rewards and learning that might occur? People at the Gore organization (a high tech manufacturer of synthetic fibers used in sportswear among other things) have an interesting way of assessing risks. They use a boat-related metaphor. Their approach goes something like this: If, in your assessment of the risk, it is above the water line on the boat, go ahead, take the risk. If you knock a hole in the boat, we can fix it without sinking. However, if you assess the risk to be "below the water line," hold off. Seek the advice of others. Share the idea more widely. Modify the idea until the risk is "above the water line."

How do we assess the level of the water line? In practice, we may have different water lines based on the nature of the issues we face and our personal risk taking propensity. To assess your water line, you might ask the following questions. If you can say "no" to each of them, you are probably above the water line.

- Is the proposed action irrevocable – once done there is no turning back?

- Is a mistake fatal – someone will be seriously harmed?

- Could the action lead to large financial losses that cannot be reduced through timely interventions?

- Is it likely that the action would lead to a significant negative response by important stakeholders?

- If the action is ineffective, will we lose much and learn little?

If it is above the water line, just do it.

---

1. Summarize an issue in two or three sentences in which you are cautious about how to proceed. What is your intended approach?

2. Is your approach risking enough? Will you learn anything if you fail? Will you learn anything if you succeed?

3. Whom do you know who seems to accurately assess the water line?

4. What would he/she say about your ideas on how to proceed? Share your ideas with her/him and ask for feedback.

5. Are you using all of the resources available to assess the water line? What might your mentor say? Ask him or her.

6 Tune in to Your Natural Discovery Process

W E EXPERIENCE millions of stimuli each day. To accommodate this onslaught of data and information, we develop ways to unconsciously guide ourselves so as not to be overwhelmed. Scientists have labeled these natural learnings "heuristics" (from the Greek, "to find out"). Consider the following areas of behavior where heuristics are common. What is your heuristic for each?

CROSSING A STREET: Some people follow the rules established by traffic authorities (i.e., following the "walk" and "don't walk" signs). But others look, estimate, and respond based on their instantaneous understanding of the traffic situation. The process of looking and estimating the likelihood of being hit or obstructing traffic is a heuristic. You do not really know how fast the drivers are traveling, nor do you know their intended movements or their focus of attention at the moment you consider crossing. But, based on your extensive past experiences, you make a judgment and take action. As each instant passes, you update your estimate. This may lead to a new judgment, or confirm the previous judgment. The process you use is a personal one. No one ever taught it to you, nor is it easy to teach to someone else. In fact, you often do not trust the "street crossing" heuristic in others, so you encourage them to follow you, or to follow the rules.

MAKING A CUP OF COFFEE:
If you are not measuring out the water and coffee grounds each time, you have evolved a heuristic for the task. If you make great coffee, you have evolved a useful heuristic formula. If your coffee is not so good, maybe some experimenting and rule-making would help.

LEARNING A NEW SPORT: Whether it be bike-riding, tennis, baseball, jogging, or ping-pong, the instruction you received (if any) is just the tip of your understanding of the sport. Through an experimenting discovery process, you began to learn the sport by doing it. You evolved heuristics around things like when to shift gears on the bike, when to run hard to get to the ball and make a tennis return (versus letting the ball go), when to slide into a base or lunge for a fly ball, how to pace yourself so that you complete the distance or avoid muscle fatigue, and when to put a spin on the ping-pong ball or when to smash it.

HOUSEHOLD CHORES: The dishes, the laundry, cooking, cleaning – you have probably developed a heuristic for each repetitive task that you do. Maybe you received instruction and now follow the rules (fat chance). What heuristics do you use? After a meal do you stack the dishes or carry them one-at-a-time? Drip dry or hand dry? Reflect on the process you use to accomplish each task. What patterns have your created? Is there a reason for the pattern? Can you learn from it on a more conscious level (you have already learned from and benefited by it on a unconscious level).

DRIVING TO WORK: There are many heuristics operating while you drive. Some of them are similar to the heuristic processes of crossing the street – you observe, estimate, judge, and act. On familiar routes you are likely to evoke many heuristics. For example, which lane do you drive in as you cross various intersections. While it may be random, it is probably more intentional than you first think. You may

stick in one lane for safety reasons, or you may move from lane to lane to keep traffic moving (most notably you). There is probably a pattern to what you do – are you aware of it? Can you learn from it and apply it to other situations?

WAKE-UP TIME: Your body clock is another heuristic. You are able to sense the time of day without the help of a clock. It may be a change in lighting, street noise, temperature, or something. Your diagnostic system is active, and you have told it when you want to get up. And it works.

As these examples suggest, we have evolved heuristic processes for many of the activities that occur with some frequency in our lives (including love making). A rigorous heuristic is a learned way of doing something that serves you well. It is not an aphorism. "He who hesitates is lost" and "Haste makes waste" do not serve as effective guides of behavior as they are contradictory.

Rigorous heuristics are learned patterns of behavior that work for us. We certainly are not thinking about all of the details surrounding an activity each time we do it. This would require too much energy, leaving too little for new tasks that require active learning. So we have developed patterns of discovered responses – heuristics that we use to simplify our lives. It may be a bit uncomfortable knowing that some part of us is guiding much of our life without our full awareness. Maybe it would be useful to have some serious (and playful) discussions with that part of you.

Some managers have told us about their "meeting man-agement" heuristics. Others have discussed their heuristics for interviewing people, handling visitors, and dealing with phone interruptions. Still others have shared their heuristics for dealing with subordinates and bosses. Many of your patterns are likely to be right for you – they will fit your style, skills, and the situation. Others may fit less well. These need to be understood so that they can be modified or replaced with more useful heuristics or more structured ways of operating that are not subject to the unconscious nature of a heuristic.

There are many benefits to tuning-in on our natural discovery processes. First, we may be able to access some of the insights that we have had on an unconscious level that relate to the various things that we do. Once these insights reach the conscious level, we can employ them more often.

Second, we can use knowledge of our patterned behaviors to more accurately diagnose our talents. If some things come naturally, look for more places where they could be used.

Third, we may be able to create a development plan to alter those heuristics that are not effective so that we become more effective. If we make lousy coffee, whether or not we measure anything in the process, it may be time to try a new process. Or if we fall prey to exaggeration, often undermining our point to those we are trying to influence, we may decide not to exaggerate – understatement may be our most powerful weapon.

The ultimate benefit of understanding our natural discovery process is the toughest benefit to gain. Can we use the pattern of patterns that we have unwittingly created in our life to get a better understanding of ourselves? This pattern of patterns may help us to gain insight into two omnipresent questions, "Who am I?" and "How do I learn?"

---

*Exploring how you develop insights
and integrate experience are the
first steps in the quest for
personal understanding.*

---

1. What patterns or heuristics do you have at
   work? Consider the following topics or tasks as
   you reflect on your behaviors:

   • scheduling or organizing a meeting
   • conducting a meeting
   • making a sales call
   • responding to a customer's complaint
   • handling unscheduled visitors
   • attending to the mail
   • responding to voice mail or electronic
     messages
   • handling a disruptive phone call
   • drafting a memo
   • reading a report

2. Where have you evolved a structured way of
   thinking about a person or situation that "kicks
   in" every time that person or situation occurs?

3. What are your standard approaches, habits,
   and operating procedures for key tasks in
   your life?

4. Are your heuristics rigorous? Do they serve you,
   or inhibit you?

7 Breaks from Expectations Can Lead to Key Learning Events

I T IS always interesting to see how much society learns from a crisis. Consider the effects of Bhopal on the chemical and safety industries, the Challenger on the aerospace industry, AIDS on the insurance and medical research industries, or the Gulf War on the global military situation. Each of these events was not expected. Each occurred because no one with sufficient authority to change the course of events was thinking such things would happen. Whether or not these events could have been prevented (i.e., controlled) is irrelevant to what can be learned now that they did happen,

Some unexpected events are disasters which start people thinking again about the safety of others and the environment. Other unexpected events are less severe – they may be breaks from the ways people have done things in the past, or they might be events that went beyond the responsible parties' ability to forecast. (Sometimes the crises are repeated a few times before the insight hits enough of the relevant people or "life repeats itself until you learn.")

Just as society often learns from its crises, we can learn from the unexpected, salient events that become part of our lives. To quote John Lennon, "Life is what happens to you while you're making other plans." It is worthwhile to take the time to learn from unexpected life events.

While such learning occurs after the event, this need not be the case. We do not need to be surprised in order to learn. We can contemplate the future through developing "what if" scenarios and conducting "threat analyses." Try asking such questions as "What can go wrong?" or "What would the situation be like if we projected the current information out 15 years?" Our work with business people suggests that only a few actively practice this approach. Most people begin thinking about a situation after it has occurred.

A personal experience brought this insight front and center. Steve was flying an airplane between Dayton, Ohio and Eastern Long Island a number of years ago. Of course when you fly or drive, there is always a chance of an accident. To overcome such fears, we tend to discount possible crisis events by thinking "it won't happen to me."

As the pilot of a Cessna 172, Steve was responsible for filing a flight plan, checking out the airplane, and flying it (including landing it safely). He describes the situation as follows.

"The trip started out well enough, then the weather got bad. Of course, I thought this might happen because I had weather reports through to my destination.

"Instead of landing, or returning to where the weather was good, I continued on route by flying between cloud

layers. Given my visual-flight-rules rating as a pilot, flying between cloud layers was a violation of FAA rules. But I was a young pilot, had passed my flight test with ease, and had about 80 hours of flying time behind me. (Not very impressive, but it seemed so at the time.)

"As I approached my refueling location, the weather had become worse. I radioed ahead to let them know I was going to land in about 20 minutes. They said, 'We have a flight emergency in progress, please circle until it has passed.' This made sense to me. I didn't want a mid-air collision as I came through the lower cloud layer to approach the airport.

"I reported in to the tower every 15 minutes or so, telling them my fuel status: '45 minutes of fuel left;' '30 minutes of fuel left;' '15 minutes of fuel left, I really must land.' The response was, 'Sorry, please hold your position. We still have an emergency in progress.' 15 minutes later, along with a few more radio communications, I was out of fuel. The propeller was standing upright in front of me. Of course, I was going down – they could not keep me up there any longer.

"I crash landed about four miles away from the airport on a street on the outskirts of Johnstown, Pennsylvania. My crisis – which I did walk away from along with my spouse in the co-pilot's seat (and we are still married 20+ years later) – was landing a plane without fuel in a mountainous region. My learnings were many, some of which I did not fully understand until years later. The more obvious learnings were that I should not have been flying between layers (the FAA got me there), that I was a skillful pilot, and that I used very poor judgment.

"I made the front page of the local newspaper – as the hero, not the fool because of my skillful landing of the plane without hurting anyone. Two eye witnesses feared for their life as I nearly went into the home of one, and almost landed on the car of the other. But my flight training paid off. I did a maneuver called 'slipping the plane' at the precise moment required to miss the house and the car on the road. The landing location was so tight that the airplane insurance company thought I was trying to commit suicide (hence they would not have to pay for the damage to the plane), until they realized that I didn't die due to skillful flying, not incompetence.

"I learned much as a result of that crisis. I learned that I could keep sufficiently calm in a crisis to perform effectively. I learned that I was not a wise pilot, that much more experience was going to be needed before I broke any more rules. I learned that many people will come to your aid in a time of crisis whom you would never guess would care. I learned that when I get 'full of myself' and feel omnipotent, that feeling is very misleading. And, I learned that seasoned pilots always report their fuel remaining, minus one hour. So when I was saying 15 minutes, the tower was thinking 1 hour and 15 minutes. They don't teach you those things in flight school."

Why do crises happen? (Why did Steve's crisis happen?) For the most part, people are comfortable with what is and think tragedy will not happen to them. "If it ain't broke, don't fix it," or "It probably will break anyway, so why do routine maintenance." Our comfort and beliefs about the future put boundaries on our thinking – creating all sorts of mental blocks that we must overcome to view a situation or person in a different way. Our experience base is not broad enough to extrapolate the information that we have to an unlikely situation. The few bits of information that we may have that could suggest an upcoming discontinuity are discarded as "outliers" – erroneous bits of information that don't belong with the rest of the data because they don't make sense based on our current way of thinking. The result is a form of myopic thinking that is only shaken by surprises.

Each time something important occurs that is a radical break from what was expected, the event carries with it many key learning points and opportunities. The event need not be negative – unexpected positive events can provide equally useful learning material. Breakthroughs in one area of science often spill over to other areas as other scientists and engineers learn of the new findings. The same appears to be true for new products. The leaps forward in most fields are the culmination of many breakthroughs, each one feeding the others.

On a personal level, you might begin to look at situations of disorder, discord, and confusion as temporary breaks in your expectations. Such situations are likely to contain many learning points if you give the situation a chance to make sense. You might put aside your expectations (which are not being met anyway) to see what follows the discord. An associate of ours calls this "the art of letting go." Letting go of a current way of thinking for a short time to see if something else might also make sense. Letting go of current ideas and assumptions permits new ideas, concepts, and knowledge to enter our mental maps of the world. This does not seem to be taught in schools – yet it seems fundamental that in life we must unlearn, as well as learn, and relearn, in order to grow and develop.

**Use unexpected events as a stimulus
to reflect, by using a different lens,
on your patterns of behavior.
Some of these patterns may
be ready for change.**

---

1. What has unexpectedly "gone wrong" in a big way at work in the past six months?

2. How do you see your work role different today in light of a recent unexpected event?

3. The Berlin Wall is down. The Cold War is over. Israel and the PLO have moved towards peace. How have these, or other significant world events, affected your expectations of your country? What Cold War patterns still exist that might be altered to benefit us and others?

8 Develop Resilience by Learning to Accommodate Adversity

S OME things just don't work out the way we plan. Our intentions are good, our analysis is well regarded. We may have made some small mistakes, but unforeseen events conspired against us. Now what?

Adversity either breaks or builds character. Coal nuggets, placed under extreme pressure, will either become dust or diamonds. To form more diamonds, we need tolerance for negative events. Manuel London defines this capability as career resilience in *Developing Managers*. One is able to bounce back, absorb the negative event, and not become downhearted, depressed, or self-denigrating. Sounds reasonable. Try to be resilient – accept the situation and move on. The next time you are passed over for promotion, are not offered the assignment you want, or do not get the size raise you feel that you deserve, focus on being resilient. In life it seems that we either get what we want, or we get an opportunity to learn something new.

In the book *Taking Charge*, Tom Mullen and Steve Stumpf discuss the idea of accommodating adversity which involves resilience and more. To accommodate adversity – adversity which will occur if we are doing anything entrepreneurial, exciting, new, or different in our lives or within our organizations – we must be able to be flexible, tolerate uncertainty, and be resilient.

Flexibility we all understand – it is doing what the other person wants. To be flexible, we need to define the alternatives to what we are currently considering, check to see if these alternatives meet with the preferencesof our "significant others," and then muster the energy and capabilities to do things differently.

Tolerating uncertainty means functioning effectively in situations that have lots of unknowns *and* which do not permit us to control when or how the unknowns are going to be explored. It is like floating in a large, turbulent body of water. Add a few undertows and bad weather to heighten the experience. A close friend, Candace Ulrich, describes her "treading water" experience this way:

> "I was on a business trip in Brazil. We had the afternoon off, so I went swimming in the ocean near the Intercontinental Hotel in Rio de Janeiro. Without warning, a wave hit me, pushed me down, and began pulling me away from shore. Within a minute I was 120 yards from shore and still being pulled out to sea. I decided to tread water rather than try to swim. I felt that the undertow and turbulence were too strong for me to make much headway swimming. I also knew that I could tread water for quite a while, maybe an hour or longer.

"The thirty minutes I was out there seemed like hours. There was no one to yell to. The ocean makes so much noise, no one would hear. The few people on shore could not see me – as I could no longer see them.

"Then a helicopter came right to where I was, lowered down a hoist, and it was over. I later asked how they saw me. The helicopter pilot didn't just happen to be flying by. Someone at the Intercontinental Hotel had seen me in the deeper water and called for assistance. After shaking a bit, and fighting back the fright, it was back to work."

Accommodating adversity involves having the strength to tolerate a negative event. Having worked with Candace in other settings, we are aware that it is a strength that she has used often. Maybe the specific water incident could have been prevented. But once it started, the ability to tolerate the uncertainty, to not give in to anxiety, and to be resilient meant the difference between success and failure. While this situation would be viewed as a crisis by many, it was not so viewed by Candace. She was a good swimmer, sailed often, and had a healthy respect for the ocean. Adversity was upon her, resilience and tolerance of ambiguity were needed. (In contrast, Steve's flight experience in Frame 7 required different abilities, and the personal meaningfulness of the crisis occurred only after significant reflection.)

Negative events challenge us all at one time or another. Some of us are not particularly good at accommodating adversity when such events occur. So we curse them. The world is not fair, or my boss is a jerk, or whatever. This does not serve us particularly well, but we convince ourselves that we feel better having said and felt it.

No single event, or even series of events, is all that life is about. Yes, it is useful to try to tolerate ambiguity, be flexible, and bounce back when things go wrong. But when these don't work for us, or when we don't have the capability to evoke them, we are stuck. When life sticks you, why not treat it as lightly as you can. You can't do much about it. Laughter is more enjoyable than anger. Accept the reality that life is unfair. No one is keeping score, there are no referees to appeal to to make things right, nor would the referees necessarily respond to your appeal if they existed. Accommodate the adversity. View it as a personal challenge to grow in ways that most cannot. Give yourself some credit for it, and enjoy the process.

Some of the best moments in life are likely to be associated with the satisfaction we feel after successfully accommodating adversity.

---

1. When recently struck by adversity, it felt great when I. . .

2. Under adverse conditions, I find myself responding by. . .

   What does your response suggest about your pattern of resilience?

3. A lesson from the "School of Hard Knocks" that I would like to share with a friend is. . .

4. Conflict is often a prerequisite to growth and development. How am I handling conflict lately?

9 Manhole Covers Are Round: Learn from the Patterns in Everyday Life

ALL HOLES are not round, but most manholes are. Did you ever wonder why? This is not likely to be a random event, nor the result of any great technological theory or expertise.

The shape of a manhole cover is simple to understand once we reflect on the purpose of a manhole and its cover. A manhole is a hole in a city street or sidewalk that is intended to permit easy human access to equipment, wires, valves or the like. In the design of the manhole, someone sensed a safety issue and asked a simple question: What can go wrong up above when someone is down below in this manhole?

The risk is that the cover falls through the hole – either on you, or on the equipment. Round covers, no matter how they are turned, will not pass through a round hole of slightly smaller diameter. This principle does not hold for most other shapes (e.g., a square cover can be inserted through a somewhat smaller square hole if the hole is entered across its diagonal).

Awareness of manhole covers is a small starting point for a grander personal understanding. Most of us spend many hours living life in a passive way; we accept what we see, hear, smell, or touch without much question. At other times, we are quite critical, rejecting much of what we experience – again, without much openness to alternatives. Manhole covers, as a metaphor for many of life's "given" situations, may help us to ask questions – sometimes of others, sometimes of ourselves.

An often told story of President Eisenhower is worth sharing: Ike was President of Columbia University after the War and before he became President of the United States. There was a particular courtyard on campus that was always being crossed by students, to the point that the grass was worn and faculty members complained to Ike and asked him to do something about it. (Does this give you an idea of what faculty members talk to their leaders about?)

Ike investigated the situation and detected the pattern. Students were taking the shortest distance between two buildings that housed their courses. The alternatives available to Ike were many: build fences to direct foot traffic, plant thorny hedges, alter classroom assignments, issue dictums and penalties for walking on the grass, ignore the issue, or pave the path. He had the path paved. Some urban planners and architects wait until the travel paths (patterns) develop, then they build the sidewalks.

When you notice a pattern, explore why the pattern exists. Let the pattern rekindle your curiosity. Sometimes you will be able to understand the pattern through an analytical or scientific answer. Other times the questioning leads to answers embedded in personal style, aesthetic preferences, tradition, culture, or values. By asking "What would make sense out of this event or situation?" *a few times*, and exploring the various answers, you may be able to understand things that you had previously ignored or accepted without question.

The patterns we see around us may be neither random nor logical. Exploring the pattern can lead us to new understandings.

---

1. What patterns do you see at work that others might not see? What might these patterns mean?

2. Why do you see them? How might you help others to see them?

3. What patterns, if any, do you see emerging within this book? What do these patterns mean to you?

10 Provability Is a Weaker Notion Than Truth

DOUGLAS R. HOFSTADTER, in his Pulitzer Prize book, *Gödel, Escher, Bach: An Eternal Golden Braid*, concludes that "provability is a weaker notion than truth" (1979, p. 19). We often cannot prove things that we know are true. How do you prove that you love someone? You may do things for them, tell them that you love them, and accommodate many things that you do not particularly care for because of this love. To you, this display of your love exemplifies the truth that you feel. Proving this to someone is near impossible. Faith and trust must suffice for proof.

Two math puzzles that were beyond proof, but alleged to reflect a truth, plagued Steve in his youth. Steve spent hours trying to figure them out. One is the three house, three utilities situation. The second relates to how many different colors are needed to color in any map without using the same color on each side of a boundary.

Try this: Draw three boxes on a page. Label them, gas, electricity, and water. Draw three houses on the page. Label them one, two, and three. Now try to connect each utility to each house without having any of the utility lines cross each other. Lines must go direct from the utility to each house (not via another utility or through another house). It does not matter where the houses or utilities are drawn on the page. The best I could get was eight uncrossed lines. The unproven truth is that all nine lines cannot be laid without at least one crossing another (in two dimensional space).

The second challenge is similar. Draw a map, or take the map of the United States. You will be able, with only four colors, to color every state (or space) such that the same color is not on both sides of a line. To my knowledge this truth has yet to be proven.

The provability-truth question is not limited to math challenges. The Fall 1991 television season covered two provability-truth stories for dozens of hours – one related to the Clarence Thomas hearings and the other the William Kennedy Smith trial. *New York* magazine and many other magazines ran cover stories on these provability-truth events. With the exception of the Iraq Gulf War media coverage, these two situations of "Men on Trial" were omnipresent for many Americans. Both ended without proving anything one way or the other. Both ended with the populace split among those that believed in several different truths. These situations and the provability-truth paradox they exemplified will be remember by most of us for many years.

What caught peoples' interest was the quest for truth (followed by justice). Who said or did what? If they said or did it, then they should be held accountable for their actions.

What intrigued the public was the efforts made to prove whatever was true. The process became a show.

What frustrated the public was knowing that we would never know the truth, and that we would believe something based on our particular points of view. Was our point of view a symptom of our prejudices or past thoughts and behaviors? Is this another provability-truth paradox on a personal level?

We are left with whatever faith we have in a system that has good intentions, along with hope and trust in our fellow humans; hope that truth wins out over provability, and trust in others that they will accept our truths when provability is not possible.

We live with a sense of personal truths, but must contend with public provability.

---

1. What personal truths do you hold most dear? List at least three.

2. How can you act on these truths at work to make you life more meaningful and satisfying?

3. What truths do you know with regard to your work situation, but which have little value because they are not shared nor provable?

4. What constitutes "proof" for your organization?

   Data?   Consensus?
   Anecdotes?   Dissension?
   Competitors' Actions?   Understatement?
   Devine Revelation?

5. Does it make a difference who offers the "proof"? If yes, what are the key attributes of the "proof" offerers?

6. What "proof" might you share for some of your more valued truths?

11 Laughter Allows One to Suspend Judgment

PSYCHOLOGISTS tell us that laughter is a natural, human response to stress. By laughing we vent the build-up of tension that a stressful event or thought is creating. Laughter frees energy that otherwise would become anxiety. Some events create so powerful a cognitive and emotional response that we have a natural means of accommodating them – we laugh. This postpones our need to confront the situation or evaluate its meaning to our lives.

Laughter not only suspends judgment, it is frequently associated with surprise, delight, and insight. It is the unexpected that we often find entertaining. Triggering an insight can bring with it an upbeat emotion, a smile, and sometimes laughter.

A professor colleague of ours who does a fair amount of after-dinner speaking has started with the following introduction on several occasions:

"Thank you for inviting me to be with you as a speaker tonight. As you know, I teach at New York University and frequently consult with businesses like yours. Some of you may be a bit hesitant to take seriously any advice that I share tonight because of the old expression, 'Those who can't do, teach.' Well, it may be worse than you think, for 'Those that can't teach, consult.' And, 'Those that can't consult, give after-dinner talks.'"

This generally gets a smile out of most, polite laughter from many, and a hearty laugh from a few. It seems to accomplish its purpose, which is to warm up the audience for what is to follow. It postpones the audiences' evaluation of the speaker for a few moments.

What is it that makes this opening humorous to people? Is it the thread of truth in the various statements, or the understatement of the speaker's capabilities? A subtle insight we see is the acceptance of different people for different tasks, with a recognition that all are necessary.

When you find yourself laughing at someone or something, you might explore why. What cord has been hit or image brought into focus? Something within you is resonating to the situation. Is it something that is important to you in a way previously unexplored? Alternatively, when you are trying to be humorous, you might reflect on some of the insights you have had to see if there is a note of humor there. I suspect that this is how Gary Larson generates new material for his *The Far Side* series.

---

*If our insights are pictures of what is,
our humor may be a frame to let
our pictures stand out.*

---

1. How and when do you use humor in the work
   place? What purpose does it serve?

2. Who recently shared a lesson with you through
   humor? What was the lesson? How might you do
   the same?

3. What role does humor play in your workplace?
   Home? Do people use humor constructively or
   destructively?

12 Analogies and Metaphors Unlock Closed Doors

CREATIVE thinking involves seeing what is there in a different way than before. "I never made any worthwhile discovery except through analogy," noted a Nobel Prize winning physicist upon receiving the honor. Rarely are new ideas the creation of something from nothing. Tom Peters supported this notion for business organizations when he stated, "a major role of the CEO is to find and share the right metaphor for the business."

A useful analogy is one that is able to suggest many of the critical aspects of a complex subject by comparison to something that is more familiar to oneself and others. For example, bureaucratic organizations are often thought of as analogous to machines. Bureaucracies and machines are generally designed to do some things well and not others. They are comprised of many interrelated parts that have defined relationships with each other. They often lack flexibility in the way that they do things, and once created, seem to have a life of their own.

Not all organizations that are viewed as bureaucracies will have all of these features to the same degree. Nor will all machines have such features to the same degree. But there is enough in common to the two entities that an analogy between the two is widely accepted. The purpose of the analogy is to help describe bureaucracy (an abstract organizational form) with something that is more familiar and concrete (machines).

Metaphors (and similes) are comparisons between two or more seemingly unrelated events or things. Metaphors can make something that is complex easier to understand by using ideas that are more familiar or graphic to the listener. The financial services industry uses a "water" metaphor for many of their technical terms: frozen assets, liquidity, cash flow, and sunk costs. The ideas of dirty money and laundering money reflect other metaphors that are linked to the water metaphor.

If an analogy or metaphor captures the essence of an issue, it is possible to develop new ways of thinking about the issue by exploring the analogy or metaphor. Consider some of the commonly used metaphors of the 1980's:

- Loose cannon (someone who is unpredictable and often damaging)

- White knight (an investor that saves a firm from take-over)

- Empty shirt (a person who looks good but has little substance)

- Golden parachute (a financial package for executives in the event of a take-over)

Or metaphors of earlier decades:

- Chip of off the old block

- Guardian angel

- From cradle to grave

- Enough rope to hang yourself

We have found metaphor to be a powerful way to develop and share insights. Read over the Table of Frames. About half of the insights shared involve the use of metaphor. To the extent that the metaphors used link to something with which you are familiar, the insight is more easily grasped and remembered.

Unfortunately, not all analogies and metaphors are strong ones. Some are able to accurately communicate more than the words themselves, others are not. Analogy and metaphor are sufficiently common in everyday communications that many of us accept them as colorful language rather than exploring the broader intentions of their user.

How far does an analogy or metaphor have to go to be a good one? A one-dimensional analogy or metaphor adds a little value to the communication. Superman was more powerful than a locomotive and faster than a speeding bullet. This colorful language makes a direct point. But each analogy stops with the one dimension identified.

Multi-dimensional analogies and metaphors have several primary linkages and are more interesting. For example, a "pyramidal organizational structure" communicates hierarchy and the relative number of people at each level of the hierarchy. There are a few powerful people at the top of most organizations, and many not-so-powerful people at the bottom. These two dimensions imply a third aspect of pyramid shaped organizations: not everyone at the bottom can rise to the top. For analogies and metaphors to unlock doors of insight, they need to have multiple dimensions.

Multi-dimensional analogies and metaphors can be intriguing. They are often developed out of one's area of specialization to clarify an emerging issue or event. When organizational theorists began to compare complex organizations to biological systems their field made a major jump forward. Both organizations and biological systems take in inputs, have a transformation process, and produce outputs. Both can regenerate themselves. Both have life cycles of birth, growth, maturity, and decline. Both are affected by and have ongoing interactions with their environments. The linkage back to what was first known in the biological sciences is a useful and powerful way to explain what is believed to be going on in organizations.

Analogies and metaphors can be taken too far. When this occurs, they break down and no longer provide the desired familiarity and understanding. This need not be a disadvantage to the use of analogies and metaphors as long as the user is aware of their limitations. In the case of the biological science metaphor, living systems do not live forever, yet organizations can (although they rarely do). The legal nature of incorporation permits an organizational entity to survive beyond the lives of its founders, suppliers, buyers, and customers. The Kodak of today involves an entirely different cast of players than the Kodak of 1880.

To unlock doors with analogies and metaphors, you will have to play with them. When you hear something unfamiliar, or want to communicate something you know a lot about to someone who is unfamiliar with the topic, look for analogies and metaphors. Find them before you proceed. Test them out on yourself – just how good are they? How many dimensions do they involve? Then, try them on a friend. Finally, use them and assist others in their use.

---

*Analogies and metaphors are bridges
that can take us from the familiar
to the unfamiliar.*

---

1. When was the last time you used an analogy or
   metaphor to explain something to someone?
   What was the analogy?

2. To expand the utility of analogy and metaphor,
   try two things:

   (a) begin to explore the meaning of the analo-
       gies and metaphors that you hear – play with
       them to see how robust they are and if they
       work for you;

   (b) look for ways to use analogies and metaphor
       in your work to communicate a difficult or
       complex idea more easily.

3. Develop these analogies and metaphors by
   identifying how they apply, and how they do
   not. Understanding others' analogies and
   metaphors opens their ideas up to you. Developing your own analogies and metaphors can
   open your ideas up to others.

4. One of management's roles is to use metaphor
   to communicate symbolically. Can you find
   metaphors that capture the essence of your work
   place?

13 Understand the Strengths of Your Senses – Line of Sight Field of Sound

WE COME to understand much of the world around us – people, places, things, and situations – by taking in data from the environment through our senses: sight, sound, touch, taste, and smell. This should not be taken to imply that all understanding is derived from the realm of the senses; people also develop understandings through their intuition, thinking, and emotions.

Acquiring data is distinct from using that data as information. How we perceive and evaluate data that we have acquired, and how we use it in making decisions, are follow-on processes to the initial acquisition process. Of interest here is how we take in data to begin with.

To the extent that the bits of data we acquire are labeled and recorded somewhere in our minds, they become the information base of our existence. Not all data taken in are labeled; our senses are assaulted all the time by stimuli that leave no marks. Nor are all data experienced necessarily recorded – our memories are rather selective of those things which we value or in which we have interest.

Even with this tremendous selectivity, we are able to develop a sizable information base by our early teens. We soon forget about our senses altogether as they seem to be doing what they are supposed to do without our thinking about them directly. Life continues along – we see more, hear more, touch more, taste more, and smell more – all the while assuming that the senses are providing us with the necessary data to function effectively.

Within the context of organizations, two senses are emphasized: visual and auditory. Something is written in a memo or report for us to see; a manager or peer talks about key ideas and entertains discussion of those ideas. If visual and auditory stimuli are most commonly used to influence what we learn in work organizations, what are the limitations of each that implicitly affect our understanding of people, places, things, and situations? Possible answers to this question lie in the phrases: line of sight, field of sound.

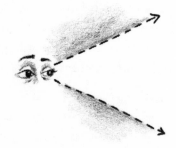

LINE OF SIGHT. A couple was walking home one night after a pleasant romantic dinner for two. A leaf blew into the woman's face and without hesitation, she raised her hand to brush it away. In so doing, she touched her eye and knocked out her contact lens. The couple immediately stopped walking, and began to look on the ground for the lens. A somewhat tipsy passerby asked what they were doing. "Looking for a contact lens," they said. The passerby walked ahead a bit until he was under a streetlight, stopped, and began looking for something. Perplexed, the couple watched him for a minute, then asked, "Have you lost something, too." "No," came the reply, "I thought I would help you look for the contact lens, and the light is better over here."

While not an original story, and probably not a true one, it captures two limitations of sight. The first is that sight is directional – we can only see in the direction we are looking. The second is that sight is greatly affected by visibility – we can only see what is not obstructed by darkness or another object. Yet, many people believe or act as if they see everything clearly. Even the most visionary among us cannot see over the horizon, through walls, or when kept in the dark. One's line of sight, however powerful it may be, is still highly constrained by reality.

Having identified two limitations to one's line of sight, we offer two ways to improve the situation. To overcome the directional limitations of sight, we have a head that can turn and feet that can propel us. The horizon is not a fixed point in space, but one that moves as we move. Our line of sight can be changed as often as we decide it is beneficial to do so. *Unfortunately, we are generally so busy developing our point of view, that we fail to recognize the limitations of our line of sight.* By moving around, both in one's physical space and mental space, we can enhance the power of our sight. Given that sight is linked to a dominant form of communication in business (i.e., the written word), understanding its limitation and actively doing things to overcome it seems prudent.

 **FIELD OF SOUND.** Steve's mother-in-law lives in a rural area near the Great Peconic Bay. He and his wife lived for many years in downtown Manhattan. When his mother-in-law visited them in New York, she brought ear plugs to deaden the city

sounds so that she could sleep. When they visited her, they were deafened by the sounds of nature – sometimes silence, other times birds or crickets.

Sounds surround us. They create a field in which we function. We cannot as easily shut sounds out as we can shut our eyes to stop seeing things. But, we do shut sounds out – often without knowing it until the situation changes or it is called to our attention. No doubt you have experienced someone calling your name quite loudly, only to respond asking, "Why are you shouting?" Or, for those with children, you find yourself saying things two or three times and wondering whether or not the child has a hearing problem. With children we often use the decibel theory, we repeat things louder.

We also use our hearing to hone in on certain sounds – a new mother can always hear her baby crying. Some mothers have said that they heard their baby stop breathing – just in time to prevent Sudden Infant Death Syndrome. Steve and his wife can be discussing something and just whisper their son's name (Eugene is 13); this same person who could not hear a direct, loud question five minutes earlier comes running in from three rooms away wanting to know what they are discussing. We train ourselves to be selective in what we hear. Are we aware of our own selective hearing, remembering, and forgetting? How can we improve our listening?

We believe the key to using sounds more productively is to first become aware of the sounds to which you listen. Instead of putting energy into not hearing all of the noise around us each day, take five minutes each day to really listen to the sounds that are there. By becoming more conscious of what is in our field of sound, we can become more attentive to the sounds that are of interest to what we are doing – we can become better listeners. Simon and Garfunkel captured this insight quite well in their song, *Sounds of Silence.*

**With such gifts as sight and hearing,
we should work on using them
to their fullest.**

---

1. What do you hear? Try it right now. Make a list
   of every sound that you hear. Can you hear
   street noises? What are they? What about house
   noises (fans, the refrigerator, clocks, television,
   the computer's hum). People noises (talk, hum-
   ming, breathing, motion)? Nature noises?

2. Close your eyes. What have you seen that is new
   or interesting today? Make a list of a few things
   at which you would like to "take a closer look."

3. Now look for the symbolism in what you have
   heard and seen today. What messages are
   intended beyond the field of sound? Line of
   sight?

4. Try this experiment at your next business meeting. Focus on one sense, then the other. What
   are the non-verbal communications saying (e.g.
   body posture, hand placement, facial expres-
   sions, dress)? What is being communicated by
   the tone of voice, pacing, and rate of speech?
   Do the words, non-verbals, and verbal manner-
   isms support a single message or are there many
   messages actually being sent?

14 Emphasize Your Dominant Sense to Enhance Your Learning

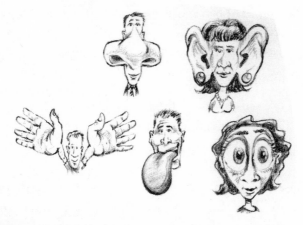

DID YOU know that most people have a dominant sense? One of their senses tends to be preferred over the others, is "on" more than the others, and has better articulation.

Think of the last time you entered an unfamiliar house or room. What struck you first: its size and lighting (spacious or small, bright or gloomy)? Or was it the sound of people talking, a fan running, music playing, or the absence of sound? What did the room smell like – can you remember this at all? What did it feel like – warm or cool, cozy or sterile, drafty or stuffy? While one does not literally taste a room, can you describe how it might taste: salty, sweet, bitter, full-bodied?

If we concentrate on the many stimuli that our senses confront, we may be able to reconstruct a rounded representation of a house or room. The senses can work in harmony if we direct them to do so. A friend has a strong auditory sense, followed by her kinesthetic sense. She detects and remembers situations most clearly by sound and feel. Her sense of smell and taste almost seem dormant. When we enter a place that has a strong smell, she does not even notice (e.g., a new car smell is entirely missed, as is the smell of garbage). Similarly with taste: different wines or chilies are hardly distinguishable – until someone with a more developed sense of taste *describes* it. By turning a gustatory message into an auditory one, she is able to appreciate the taste of things more fully.

Of the five senses, one of three is a preference of over 95 per cent of the American population (if you believe survey data and statistical analysis): sight, sound, and touch. This means that whatever information is retained by us is primarily represented by either visual, auditory, or kinesthetic messages in the brain. The concepts and research on neurolinguistic programming support this premise. The majority of Americans have a visual preference, about one third have an auditory preference, and less than 10 per cent have a kinesthetic preference.

Our dominant sense is our preferred sense; we will think about and do things with it more often than with the others when given free choice. We will remember people, places, things, and situations through this sense more easily and more frequently. For example, think of the last person you met. What came to mind first: the face or body? the name or voice? the handshake?

Visually dominant people tend to remember through visualizations: pictures, flashbacks, graphics, maps, and scenery. Auditory dominant people remember through sounds: voices, music, sayings, speeches, and lectures. Kinesthetic dominant people remember through feelings: touch, movement, and intensity.

Having a sense preference does not mean that the other senses are inactive, nor that they can not be highly developed for some situations. It would be like two people attending the same movie, one with a dominant visual sense, the other with a dominant auditory sense. One remembers the pictures and can use them to recreate aspects of the movie; the other remembers the sound track and can use the music and words.. When the visual and audio tracks of a movie are well synchronized, there is a shared event for future discussion. But if the visual and audio are not telling the same story, the two people will remember a different movie.

To diagnose a dominant sense (you probably have one), consider the following possible ways (called modalities) of remembering some person, place, thing, or situation. Which seem to reflect the ways that you remember most often? On the following page, rate the items in each list on a scale from "1" to "5."

1 —————— 2 —————— 3 —————— 4 —————— 5
Infrequent   *Moderately Frequent*   *Very Frequent*

In doing the ratings, think of a specific person first. How do you remember him or her? Then think of a place. What comes to mind? Finally, think of a situation that was significant to you. With these thoughts in mind, rate each word below from "1" to "5." Now, total the ratings.

Your highest total is likely to be your dominant sense. The greater the difference in the totals, the greater the strength of the dominant sense. The maximum one could score on any sense is 60; the minimum is 12. Scores above 45 reflect a preference.

Visual	Auditory	Kinesthetic
Still Pictures	Words	Feelings
Relative Positions	Music	Texture
Colors	Volume	Vibration
Moving Pictures	Cadence	Intensity
Sizes	Inflections	Heaviness
Self In/Out of Pic.	Tempo	Movement
3-D quality	Pauses	Pacing
Contrasts	Uniqueness	Duration
Angle of View	Rhythm	Density
Shapes	Soundtracks	Hot/Cold
Focus	Emotion	Pressure
Brightness	Pitch	Muscle Tension
TOTALS		

Having identified ones dominant sense, now what? The most important thing that we have discovered is that different kinds of media have a significant impact on us and our ability to remember. If your dominant sense is visual, then what you see is what you get. Information presented visually will be understood and remember by visually dominant people better than information that is only presented orally. When we are working with others, we ask people to show us what they are talking about. We invite them to draw a picture, make a graph, sketch the relationships between the key causes of an event; provide a picture, pie chart, icon, or whatever captures their thoughts and words as pictures. At a minimum, we ask for a copy of their ideas in writing (a memo, report, written summary, minutes of the meeting), or we make a written or graphic summary of their ideas ourselves. The worst thing we could do is leave the event without a visual representation.

If your dominant sense is auditory, then what you hear is what you'll remember. Be sure that you check for understanding with the other participants in any meetings, because if you misunderstand, follow-up written communications will probably not correct the misunderstanding. When you receive written or graphic communications, call the sender to discuss the topic. Have the sender talk you through his thoughts.

If your dominant sense is kinesthetic, you will best remember things that you experienced directly. You need to be part of an event to best understand the ideas presented. You may even have to experience the event first-hand to comprehend its significance. It is when you get into the driver's seat, speaker's suit, salesperson's shoes, or athlete's jersey that the tactile part of the event is experienced. Take every opportunity possible to be where the action is, and be a part of that action. You need to go on those sales calls, be a part of those task forces or staff meetings, and go to the ball park or opera. Much of what you remember will be the tactile sensations that you experienced – the vibrations of the crowd roaring, the coolness of the night air, the rumble of the subway, or the comfort of your seat. These sensations will anchor the experience.

Once we have begun to leverage our dominant sense to attain and better remember information, we may want to apply our knowledge to others. What is the dominant sense of your spouse or partner, boss, child, or other significant person in your life. Your communications with these people can be enhanced if you can tune into their dominant sense (or if they can tune into yours). If the audience is primarily visually-oriented, give them pictures, graphics, sketches, cartoons, or whatever they will resonate to most easily. If the audience is more auditory-oriented, say it loud and clear and often. Add music or other auditory backdrop to what you are doing to reinforce the messages you are sending. If the audience is more kinesthetic, get them involved. Get them talking, singing, clapping, standing, walking, stretching, and whatever else is not clearly inappropriate to the situation.

Just how strong is one's dominant sense, and just how different might people be as a result of dominant sense differences? Steve's dominant sense is visual; his wife's is auditory. While there may be may explanations for their differences, sense preferences explain some of them.

Preferences	Steve (Visual)	Maria (Audio)
DATING ACTIVITY	Movies	Jazz Clubs
HOME ENTERTAINMENT	TV	Stereo/Radio
DAY DREAMS	Pictures/Cityscapes	Music/Songs
LEARNING MODE	Reading/Self Study	Lectures
COMMUNICATIONS	In Writing	By Tel./In Person
VACATION	Sites to Remember	Clubs to Remember
HOBBIES	Cars/Antiques	Piano/Perform. Arts
WORK	Tangible, Things	Interactive, People

I saw, I heard, I did. But what do I remember? What will they remember?

---

1. What is your dominant sense?

   your partner's?   your manager's?
   your mother's?   your daughter's?
   your father's?   your son's?

2. Reflect on these relationships. How are they affected by differences in sense preference?

3. Pick one relationship to enhance in your next interaction. How can you more closely link to their dominant sense – and in so doing, broaden your sensitivity?

4. In preparing for your next presentation, identify three ways of communicating that use a better balance of the three dominant senses.

5. Describe a vivid memory, either on paper or on tape. Let yourself go; be as elaborate as you can. When this is done, examine your choice of words in describing this memory. Which sense is dominant? Does this support your earlier ratings of key phrases? If not, what might explain the difference?

15 Develop Your Creativity, Your Intellect Will Follow

DURING early childhood we encourage creativity. The unusualness of a drawing leads to appreciation by teachers and family. By fourth grade, reading, writing, and arithmetic replace exploring, drawing, and creating as the main topics at school each day. It is a rare school and home life that reinforces the creativity of youth in the middle school and high school years.

Unless we pursue a research or arts-oriented profession, the majority of our college education and work experiences focus on expanding our knowledge base and intellect rather than our creativity. Implicit in this focus is that creativity is not as important as is knowledge, and that creativity is not essential to succeed in work or life. The "right" way has been determined by someone else. What we need to do is understand these "right" ways and replicate them at appropriate times.

This approach may be efficient for organizations and situations that rarely need to change. If the environment is stable and predictable, and competitors are docile, doing more of the same without changes or improvements eliminates costly mistakes. It also eliminates trial and error learning.

Most organizations today are not in such situations – or at least not for long. Yet a *learned* resistance to creativity and change dominates many of us. Because we have been socialized and rewarded for conforming for two decades (early adult life, ages ten to thirty), and frequently shunned or criticized for not conforming, it is likely that our creativity skills are rusty. When ingenuity and resourcefulness are needed, we distrust our creative energy and may be slow to act. We often fail to provide the organizations that we work and live in with ideas and ingenuity to figure out how to get the tough tasks done in less time at less expense; or the resourcefulness to figure out how to bring the people, finances, and inspiration together to make changes happen.

Creativity does not appear to come easily to many professionals. Yet, these same people have many of the characteristics associated with creative people. Many professionals are:

- open to experience and the ideas of others
- able to see things in alternative ways
- curious
- accepting of apparent opposites

- persuasive, persistent, and thorough
- in need of and assuming autonomy
- independent in judgment, thought, and action
- tolerant of ambiguity and comfortable with change
- flexible, yet clear on direction
- responsive to feelings
- able to think in images
- able to concentrate
- able to generate a large number of ideas
- willing to take risks

If we have many of these abilities and characteristics, why is it that we rarely see ourselves as creative people and hesitate to suggest creative ideas? What is lacking is the motivation to be creative. This motivation involves a willingness to try new things, propose atypical ideas, and develop uncommon associations between events and situations. It would require that we let go of some of our current ways of thinking and denounce some of our hard-earned knowledge, to make room in our minds to let in some new ideas. As Roger von Oech suggests in his book, *A Whack on the Side of the Head*, we all need a whack now and then to break our patterns of thinking in order to permit ourselves to think about things differently. Whacks come in many colors and flavors – consider the use of humor, sarcasm, non sequiturs, puns, "what if" scenarios, debate, and point-counterpoint discussions.

This ability to think about things differently was demonstrated to Steve vividly at an early age. It has stuck with him ever since. When he was eight years old Steve attended a family gathering – a clam bake – with several dozen of his parent's friends and relatives. During the meal (a clam bake lasts for hours) his Dad decided that he would orchestrate a playful event. He had recently been the subject of this activity and had a pressing desire to try it out himself on an audience. He obtained a bed sheet and some kind of hat. He draped the sheet over his shoulders and announced that he was the "Great Swami of Siam." We had no idea what this was about, but if he wanted to wear a sheet and hat and make a fool of himself, we would play along.

Dad explained to those who were listening (about half of the audience), that he was a great spiritual leader. They too could experience a wondrous spiritual experience, if they followed his direction. He had a chant that they must say while on their knees, bowing to him. They were to repeat the chant while they bowed, then come back to the upright position. Then chant and bow again. They were to repeat this process until they received a special spiritual message that would be conveyed to them through his special powers. When they thought that they had received this message, they were to raise their hand, and then convey the message to the Great Swami of Siam in private.

The whole thing was silly enough to get some takers. Not everyone got on their knees at the same time, but over the next hour nearly everyone did – a total of 24 dutiful subjects in all. The chant that each was to say, in unison with the others that were participating, was "Oh waa, ta goo, Siam." Try it. Say "Oh waa, ta goo, Siam" out loud a few times.

So there we were, chanting, "Oh waa, ta goo, Siam." How long this was to continue until the spiritual message was received we did not know. After five minutes, one person thought that they had received the message. Apparently not, as my Dad instructed them to continue the chant. Then someone else thought that they got it. And they did. We all clapped, and wondered what was wrong with us. One by one we began to see the familiar in the unfamiliar (what the chant was really saying), and the unfamiliar in the familiar (what my Dad was really up to). The chant, "Oh waa, ta goo, Siam" when spiritually received, is enunciated, "Oh what a goose I am." We all had a great time, laughed at ourselves, and saw some simple creativity in action.

In order to free ourselves from this practical joke, we had to think differently about something that we were doing. The actual repetition of the chant worked against thinking about the situation differently, as did the physical motion of bowing. We were locked into one interpretation of the situation based on our initial perception of the task. We were trapped by our intellect and the habitual behavior required by the exercise – we were hooked into one way of thinking and doing based on the simple instructions provided. If this happens easily, and for something that we realize is a ruse, might it be happening unconsciously much of the time?

Develop your creativity, your intellect will follow. The world's geniuses in most fields of endeavor have exhibited highly creative behavior. Often because of this they are considered to be some of the world's most brilliant people. But, which came first, you might ask – the creativity or the brilliance? It was the creativity that came first – the ability to see in the familiar the unfamiliar; and in the unfamiliar, the familiar. They could experience the same things as others, but think something differently.

This should not be taken to imply that every creative thought is of great value; most are not. It is through creating and considering alternatives that new possibilities can be pursued. And it is the consideration of the alternatives that develops the intellect. Knowledge is gained from considering the ideas that subsequently lead to successes, as well as those ideas put aside as not viable. The intellect does follow.

Knowledge accrues fastest to those who consider many possibilities; they gain knowledge from both what they choose to do and what they choose not to do.

---

1. What new or different idea have you pursued lately?

2. What was the last belief that you put aside for a new or alternative one?

3. When are you most creative (e.g., mornings, after lunch, before sex [how is that for a whack on the side of the head], while doing a routine task, late at night)? How can you leverage this knowledge to yield more creative ideas on work tasks?

16   *The Spirit of Diagnosis Is Discovery*

WE HAVE been taught many concepts and skills throughout our lives, ranging from history and literature, to math and science. But in most of the teaching to which we were exposed, and in much of the learning that we accomplished, the skill of diagnosis was presented as analysis. The mysteries to be resolved were expressed as problems to be solved.

Diagnosis is different from analysis. Diagnosis involves emotion and curiosity. While analysis may be dry and methodical, diagnosis is often exciting and adventurous. Diagnostic skills involve estimating, examining, probing, and unraveling, whereas analytic skills involve logic and reasoning.

Reflect on the tools often used by the people we hire to diagnose something, e.g., a medical doctor. Doctors use all sorts of examining and probing tools. They collect information on many different human systems as part of their general exploration of most ailments as a way to unravel what may be wrong (e.g., measures of blood temperature and pressure, respiratory sounds and flows). They ask the patient to estimate the seriousness of the ailment by touching here and poking there and inquiring how much does it hurt, and so forth. They then take the information obtained from their diagnosis and analyze it. Their analysis feeds into their previous experience and intuitive-based curiosity to help confirm or question their sense of what is really happening within a particular patient.

Effective diagnosis requires us to ask appropriate questions, look in some areas for information, and ignore other areas. A doctor who collects the wrong diagnostic information may have great difficulty in reaching an accurate prognosis based on his or her analysis of that information. Good diagnosticians are curious and interested in finding something out. They like to resolve the mystery of the situation.

In work situations we are generally provided with symptoms of some problem as a stimulus for action. Sometimes symptoms get treated as if they are the problem, or the symptoms are used as the appropriate information for analysis. Symptoms are best considered as a starting point for active diagnosis. Symptoms are the clues that spur the next steps – an exploratory process to resolve the present mystery.

A large food manufacturing and marketing organization was recently confronting a decline that substantially exceeded projections in its sales of one of its traditional dry breakfast cereals. This particular cereal's niche had been attacked by two competitors and there had been a proliferation of new dry breakfast cereals launched within the past two years. This information, when used to analyze the situation, resulted in the conclusion that the lost market share was due to increased competition.

The advertising manager on this cereal's account knew that the ads for the cereal were testing at the same level of consumer awareness. Generally, awareness levels and purchases moved together: decreases in awareness would be followed by decreases in purchases. Since consumers seemed to still know about the product, why had they reduced their purchases? This was a bit mysterious to her. She asked her assistant account manager to request the market research staff to conduct a short phone survey of about 100 people to get a quick sense of the market. Based upon what consumers said, a more rigorous study would be done or the issue would be dropped.

In her review of the research, the assistant account manager noted that on two occasions consumers responded that they thought the cereal didn't taste as good as it used to taste. Yet, she knew of no change in the cereal's ingredients or manufacture. She became curious and explored the situation further with the client's assistant product manager.

As the inquiry proceeded to resolve the mystery, it was discovered that about eight months earlier the client had been testing some different salt levels for this product in specific test markets. While the decision was made not to alter the salt level, no one had communicated this to production. The last salt level used in a market test was now being used as the standard across all markets. With this mystery resolved, the salt level was immediately returned to its appropriate level. Within a few months sales began to move upward; by the end of the year they had returned to their projected level.

By treating the decline in sales as a symptom, rather than the problem, the assistant account manager decided to seek more information; to explore. This exploration led to the eventual definition of the problem – less desirable taste – which was easily corrected.

Diagnosis includes technical analysis as a tool in the discovery process. There were numerous clues available to the cereal manufacturer that did not fit together. Some straightforward analysis was performed. By itself, this analysis was of little use and may have misled future decisions had it not been examined further.

Within an analytic framework, we tend to identify the best fit possible (i.e., analyze the data) and conclude something logical based on that fit. But what if key data are missing? It is asking this question that helps us shift to a more diagnostic framework from the previous analytic one. If our analysis uses only the symptoms received, and we do not treat key issues as mysteries to be resolved, we may well reach an unwise solution – in a perfectly logical, rational way.

***Without an active discovery process,
our analysis of key issues may be
logically correct based on the
information available, but its
usefulness may be minimal.***

---

1. What was the last mystery that you resolved?
   Was it the result of detailed analytic thinking, or
   a fluid process of exploration, thought, counter-
   thought, and discovery?

2. Identify two or three "problem areas" at work
   that need to be explored. Conceptualize these as
   mysteries to be resolved, rather than problems to
   be solved.

17 Completing Crossword Puzzles Exemplifies Much of What People Find Frustrating in Business

THE LAST time Joel was working on a crossword puzzle he began to explore the process he was using to complete it. Where did he start? It was not with "1-across". (He read this clue, but did not know the answer.) He started with 4-down. Since there was no one correct place to start, he started where it was easiest for him. He then focused his efforts on a small section of the puzzle trying to respond to both the across and down clues until he got stuck. Then he moved to another section of the puzzle with the intent of coming back to the earlier section when he acquired some additional insight. He changed his mind on several occasions and needed to erase two previous answers. He found a few words in the dictionary (he is no purest), and he asked his spouse for help. He put the puzzle down to eat lunch, and went back to it several hours later.

Joel describes the process of completing a crossword puzzle as enjoyable and challenging. It was in reflecting on its non-linear, iterative, messy nature that a realization occurred – this is the kind of process that we often complain about at work. Projects sometimes get off to a false start – or do not get started at all while someone is waiting for one more piece of data or someone's approval. People do not know where to begin when trying to resolve the really tough issues, so they either start where it is easiest for them, or postpone the task. When people do begin, they often have to change approach several times before the job is done. It is also particularly bothersome to some people that there is no single right way to resolve many of the issues they confront.

The process of completing a crossword puzzle has many of the same attributes as managerial work. It may *not* be the process *per se* that leads to frustration, but the failure of the linear, structured approach that we expect to materialize. Why do people anticipate a structured, linear process for resolving complex, business issues? We suspect that it is because they never thought much about it. They simply transfer the step-by-step analytic frameworks taught in school to live business situations.

A business associate of ours was recently involved in a decision to launch a new product and the decision's subsequent implementation. The analysis conducted was extensive: an elaborate market segmentation study was conducted, detailed product design and manufacture specifications were created, focus groups were hired to discern possible customer reactions to samples of the product, and so on.

While there were many stops and starts throughout the year on all aspects of the product launch, management held fast to its original goal and approach. Unfortunately, some of the information obtained along the way did not fit nicely into the original new product business plan. Some of the answers to emerging clues to their "crossword puzzle" did not fit with other answers. Management had many options, as the product was not yet on the market. But, the original plan was to be followed as it was based on good data and good analysis; more current, less rigorously collected information was essentially ignored.

The product did significantly less well in the market than expected. Yet information was clearly available that could have been used to alter aspects of the product launch to make it more successful. One of the reasons why this information was not used effectively was because in had not entered the process at the "appropriate" time. Clearly revokable decisions were viewed as irrevocable. The train was on the track and moving ahead. The non-linear and convoluted nature of ill-structured decision situations was ignored.

The fact that many business situations do not lend themselves to linear frameworks is frustrating. Once it is accepted that business problem-solving and decision-making are messy processes, it is easier to cope with and enjoy the ill-structured nature of our work.

---

*Organizing something that defies
structure is frustrating – so why bother?
Messy is messy, it need not
be frustrating.*

---

1. Is your office messy or neat? Is this driven by you or the nature of your work?

2. Reflect on a major work or personal change that you voluntarily have undertaken. How orderly or messy was the process that you used to make the decision?

3. To what extent did you go with your energy in making and implementing this decision? Was it a FLOW experience (see Frame 2).

4. Was it a comfortable or frustrating experience? What would you do differently?

18 Don't Ask the Question if You Can't Live With the Answer

A FEW years ago an employee of a large consumer electronics firm shared the following story of an earlier career situation that he felt he handled poorly. At the time, he (let's call him Pete) was the manager of a remote sales center that was partially computerized. Sales personnel would call in to this center for price quotes, quantity availability, shipping times, and the like (this was before these functions were fully automated). The twenty plus people working the phones were able to access the information on a computer terminal and report it to the sales personnel.

The morale among the telephone clerks was at an all time low. Turnover was high, absenteeism was common, tardiness occurred with half the staff nearly every day. Worst of all, the errors created by the staff made the company look incompetent to the buyers.

When Pete asked his employees what was wrong, he got answers like, "this job is boring", "there is no career advancement potential out of this job." Absenteeism and tardiness excuses were often: "I have other commitments too, you know, I have a family and children." "I arrived late because the bus came late for my kids to go to school. I couldn't leave them home alone." Or, "I had a doctor's appointment on Friday, that's why I wasn't here."

Pete tried everything he could think of to improve morale and reduce the attendance problems. Nothing worked. One of the workers suggested that he consider instituting a flextime program. This would allow people to sign up for specific schedules that met their personal needs. Everyone would still work the peak hours of 10:00 a.m. to 3:00 p.m. each day, but the fringe hours would be covered by a subset of employees based on their individual (and group) preferences.

Pete thought the idea was reasonable, but felt that he lacked formal authority to institute it. So he did what many would do, he asked his boss at headquarters for permission to try a flextime program. His boss asked Personnel. Personnel came back with an answer like this: "If we allow Pete to offer flextime at his office, we will have to offer it everywhere. What if other's find out about it, they may all want it. We need to study this before you give permission to alter the official work schedule." In short, "no, don't permit it." Pete's boss said no. Pete told the employees that he had tried to get the flextime arrangement, but that management said "not now" because they wanted to study the idea further before trying it in any units.

Things went from bad to worse. Turnover increased, seven people left within the next two weeks. Attendance and absenteeism remained high. Quality did not improve. Pete was finally moved to another unit at headquarters where management could "oversee the development of some of his management skills."

What went wrong? By asking permission, Pete set himself up for an answer he could not live with. Once an answer was given, in this case, "no, you cannot try a flextime program," Pete was stuck. If he tried one anyway, no matter how successful it may initially appear, management would chastise him for being insubordinate, undo the flextime program, and thereby make matters worse. By following management's direction, Pete was left out on a limb with nowhere to go. His employees didn't really believe him when he said he had passed the buck upstairs. What little chance of influencing their behaviors that he had was sacrificed to the rules of the bureaucratic system.

Pete left this position frustrated and angry. But he gained an important insight: Do not ask the question if you cannot live with the answer. Of course there are potentially negative consequences associated with not asking permission when permission is generally required before taking actions. What must be weighed is the cost of a negative answer against the consequences associated with not asking permission.

"Don't ask the question if I can't live with the answer" is most appropriate when you are at a remote location (or on the midnight to 8:00 am shift) such that you are expected to exercise discretion in your actions. It also is appropriate when the organization or workgroup has a climate that espouses empowerment, decentralized decision-making, or experience-based professional development.

It is easier to ask for (and get) forgiveness than it is to get permission.

---

1. By not asking for permission, you are increasing your personal risk. Identify two issues in which you could ask for permission or approval before proceeding. Just how big is the risk that you would take if you proceeded without getting approval? (Are the punctures that may occur above or below the water line? See Frame 5.)

2. How will it feel if your are denied permission? What effect will a "no" decision have on your people?

3. It is easier to take actions and risk mistakes if you have a reasonable power base. Is your personal power base such that forgiveness is likely? How might you find out? Who might you see for guidance rather than permission?

4. Apologizing for a mistake is an important communication skill. When was the last time that you practiced this skill?

19 Use an Action–Learning Process to Lead Change: Plant, Prune, Graft, and Proliferate

THE direction of major change in social systems is generally from the empowered core to the periphery of the
organization. That is, after extensive analysis and delib-
eration, a programmatic response from headquarters is rolled
out to the field. This approach does *not* imply that the
empowered core has diagnosed the need for change, or that
they have developed the new ideas and methods that are to
replace the old. Both issue diagnosis and the design of
possible solutions might have been surfaced by those outside
of the empowered core, e.g., in a production unit, by the sales
force, or through customer service activities. But once the
need for change is apparent and the change program has
been designed, the empowered core commands and directs
the change process.

An alternative to this top-down tradition is an action-learning approach for dealing with change that reverses the direction of control. In the action-learning approach, the periphery of the organization serves as the leading edge for the firm as a whole. The action-learning at this leading edge reduces the need for the empowered core to conduct extensive analyses and deliberations – programmatic response from headquarters is not necessary. It is the grass roots forces throughout the organization, represented by those with direct contact with customers, suppliers, buyers, and other key stakeholders, that initiate the firm's change process. The empowered core's role is to guide and facilitate change, not command and control it. Policy development relies more on local experience than on core expertise.

This probably sounds interesting, particularly to those not part of the empowered core. But how can it work? Why should those with power relinquish it to those with local experience? In practice, they do not. They do not give up their power, nor do they continually exercise it to control the change effort. They retain their power, but exercise it less often as they permit others to use local experience as a basis for action.

This distinction between having power and using it is at the root of all empowerment approaches to management.

The empowered core assumes the role of a caretaker of the living systems. Much like the owners of a nursery, they work with their employees to nurture the growth of their products. The empowered core collaborates with the peripheral units – planting, pruning, grafting, and proliferating the healthiest fruits of their labor.

PLANTING. Planting is a grass roots event. Something occurs in a business that needs a response – such as a valued employee leaving the organization unless an unusual form of work schedule flexibility can be arranged. The formal policies do not apply, or if applied, will not resolve the situation satisfactorily. Rather than force a policy decision, a pilot program is created. A pilot program is not simply an exception to the rules.

To be a part of a pilot program means that the local unit designs a response to the situation that:

- meets the specific needs of the individual(s) and local situation, and
- meets the more general learning needs of the organization as a whole.

A seed is planted under a special set of conditions, and local managers have agreed to monitor the seed's growth to see if they can learn from what has been planted.

PRUNING. Local responsiveness does not inherently mean firmwide adaptability. If deviations from past practices were not a part of pilot programs, local initiatives would represent exceptions to firm policy rather than a stage in policy development. A large organization could soon be overgrown with exceptions. The pruning stage acts to prevent program overload, and to channel local programmatic responses into uncovering larger policy issues for the organization. Pruning means that as a pilot effort sprouts, the local unit and headquarters staff jointly evaluate it. Some initiatives will be allowed to continue, and others will be cut. Through careful pruning, growth in the number and diversity of new programs is managed.

GRAFTING. Grafting is the art and science of crossbreeding. The evaluation of a pilot program can lead to new understandings of what can work under specific conditions. As the organization reviews many different pilot efforts, it may become desirable to crossbreed some of the better ideas learned through the pilot efforts. Grafting is different that sowing the same seeds in new places – which amounts to planting similar pilot ideas in different units. Grafting is taking the best aspects of different pilots and combining them in a new way not previously considered. As most gardeners know, grafting does not always work. Sometimes the unique strengths of two different plants lead to a new plant with the strength of neither. Sometimes a new plant will not even bud as the grafting was unsuccessful. Yet, grafting can lead to crops that are stronger, more robust, and more useful to their growers. Grafting should be part of the action-learning cycle.

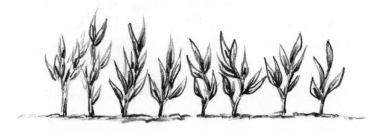

PROLIFERATING. Once an initiative has shown promise at one site, further testing at other sites is often desirable. Just how generalizable is the new idea? What are its limitations? Only when an initiative demonstrates that it is transplantable elsewhere in the organization does change in firmwide policy become practical. For many reasons, diffusing innovation in large organizations is difficult (and slow!). Traditional hierarchies are designed to foster communication up and down, not across functions and business units. The "not invented here" syndrome slows awareness of what is happening in other parts of the organization.

The grass roots approach can foster proliferation in several ways. The groundwork for proliferation can be established at the beginning of the pilot program. The initiating unit can be put in touch with other units known to be addressing a similar issue. Successful pilot programs can be rewarded and recognized by headquarters, thereby encouraging others to both attempt pilots and share in others' successes. Headquarters can develop a clearinghouse of successful pilot efforts, reporting them in the company newsletter, at policy meetings, and the like.

Coopers & Lybrand, an international public accounting and management consulting firm, has been experimenting with the plant, prune, graft, proliferate action-learning process. One area of particular concern has been to address issues derived from their workforce's diversity (e.g., employees and clients who vary in gender, age, race, nationality, culture, religion, language skills, behavioral patterns, career issues, family situation, and so forth).

With scores of public accounting and consulting offices worldwide (referred to as "practice offices"), Coopers & Lybrand is continually confronted with conflicting demands for long-term centralized planning and short-term decentralized action. Each practice office must stay in touch with the needs of its clients, the economic needs of the office, and the needs of its office employees; each has significant autonomy in how it achieves these responsibilities.

In terms of workforce diversity, as particular needs arise that are not addressed by traditional firm policy, the practice offices are encouraged to develop action-learning programs. The requirements for such efforts are for the practice office to:

- develop an initiative they believe will be responsive to their needs;

- work with headquarters to create the parameters of a local pilot effort,

- participate in evaluating the initiative after a specified period of time and decide whether to continue it;

- cooperate with other practice offices working on similar issues; and

- participate in a firmwide recognition process.

National headquarters of Coopers & Lybrand plays a parallel role to that of the practice office in the plant, prune, graft, proliferate action-learning process. In addition to overall management responsibility, national headquarters:

- develops annual status reports on workforce diversity issues in the firm;

- solicits input from the workforce on diversity and other issues biannually through a firmwide employee survey;

- researches workforce diversity issues and looks for ways to aid practice offices in their individual initiatives;

- connects the local practice office proposing an initiative with other offices known to be addressing that issue, as well as to external resources with relevant expertise;

- works with the practice office to design the parameters of the pilot program;

- co-evaluates the pilot program after a specified period of time;

- designs and facilitates the workplace innovations recognition process; and

- codifies the experience of the firm into workforce diversity policies.

Through its action-learning efforts, Coopers & Lybrand is applying a grass roots approach to its business challenges.

To promote action-learning, decentralize initiatives while centralizing the diffusion of successes.

---

1. Where are the roots of the majority of initiatives in your organization today – the field or headquarters? Why?

2. Which successful field initiatives could benefit the organization through application in other areas?

3. What can headquarters do to stimulate local or field initiatives?

4. What might be inhibiting headquarters from stimulating local or field initiatives? How might you influence headquarters to change their approach?

20 The Sweet Spot in Life Is Satisfying What We Want, What They Want, and What We Can Do – All at the Same Time

OUR work with hundreds of individuals in management development programs led us to understand some of the personal discoveries that they had made (which they sometimes had difficulty articulating to others). In listening to their views of what is effective management, we were able to identify three interrelated sets of ideas which continually need to be identified, attended to, and acted upon: business and individual goals, the goals of significant others that could affect your business or personal life, and business and individual capabilities.

The lack of business and individual goals is frequently identified by people as one reason for their current problems. Do any of the following statements sound familiar?

- "What we need around here is a better sense of direction."

- "What is it that my boss really wants, anyway. If he were more clear, I could do my job a whole lot better."

- "If my boss had given me more guidance on what she wanted, I would have finished this two days ago."

- "Every year we focus on something different – so why bother trying to keep up, things will change again next year."

The inability to understand or satisfy the goals of significant others is a second reason that people identified for things not progressing as planned. People have probably made comments such as these to you:

- "I need more buy-in on this idea. Why won't production loosen up a bit?"

- "I can't seem to get any real support for this product. Marketing is dragging its heals."

- "This project would have really flown if the organization had gotten behind it. But without the continued R&D support, its going to be a 'too little, too late' product."

The lack of business and/or individual capabilities is a third explanation given for the some of the problems confronted. The following reasons are representative of the explanations given for why a project will not be approved or completed on time:

- "We need $2 million to launch this repositioning campaign and no one will free up the funds."

- "The new building will cost $70 million over the next two years. I know we are not going to get corporate's okay on this."

- "We need to hire four more engineers if we are going to make any headway on this project. We'll never find ones as talented as the ones we just lost."

These ideas, when reflected in simple language, deal with: What do you want, what do others want, and what are you capable of doing? We pose these ideas as three questions to be continually asked and answered throughout your life:

What do you want? What do they want?
What can you do?

To capture the diagnostic and discovery value of these questions, we associate each question with a circle in Figure 1. Each circle signifies the ideas and behaviors that are possible answers to one of the questions. While the circles could be positioned anywhere in the figure, there is a meaning to the limited overlapping placement that is shown. Figuratively, you would record your answers to each question in that question's circle. The objective is to identify courses of action that satisfy the questions in all three circles simultaneously.

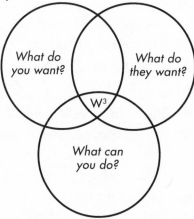

Figure 1. The W–Cubed Model

Out of your initial answers to each question separately come new insights as to how you could proceed more effectively. The answers may be idiosyncratic to your situation, but the process of asking these questions and reflecting on the answers is a general one. The answers guide behavior in much the same way as a physician's diagnostic questions guide the physician's behavior. The patient's responses to his physician's questions and actions provides information that may lead to discovery and additional questions.

We have labeled the model shown in Figure 1 as W^3 (W-cubed) to signify the three "What" questions that you need to ask yourself repeatedly in your leadership efforts. Using set notation, W^3 is shown as three overlapping circles. The overlap among the circles is the sweet spot of this diagram. The sweet spot is intended to suggest that the most effective ideas will be simultaneously addressing the three diagnostic questions: What do we want? What do they want? and What can we do?

The W x W x W symbolism is also intended to communicate the importance of simultaneously answering all three diagnostic questions. As with any equation involving only multiplication, if any of the elements is zero, the product is zero. Finding answers to each of the three questions that are consistent and compatible with the answers to the other two questions is critical to your thinking. Let's explore each of these diagnostic questions.

WHAT DO WE WANT? Organizational and individual goals define the set of valued outcomes that you intend to seek. The question of whose goals are going to be accomplished by attending to various issues is a critical question. Within the context of the W^3 model, you are asking the question, *Who is we?"* It is common and necessary for you to have more than one point of reference when thinking about issues.

Reference points might be thinking about the situation as the manager of the business unit, as someone's subordinate, as a peer of other managers, as a mentor to one or more of the workers, and possibly as a member of a committee, task force, or planning group. You are probably responsible for activities that go beyond any single individual's wants. What you want for yourself in your career may be different than what others want in the position they occupy. By asking the question "*Who is 'we'?*" you are able to focus your diagnosis on a single entity at a time. "We" could be "you" personally. "We" could also be you as a manager in your organizational position. "We" could be the entire business unit, or the entire organization. As you may suspect from the large number of "we's," the W³ model is best applied to one "we" at a time. It can then be reapplied to other "we's" that reflect your different perspectives on an issue.

The process of identifying what you want may also take the form of eliminating what you do not want, by eliminating some alternatives that are not consistent with your goals. It is easier for some people to identify the things that they do *not want* because this can be accomplished by reflecting on policy statements and past actions to identify the not-so-successful situations and events. To determine what is wanted in the future requires knowing or envisioning possibilities – something that some people find hard to do.

Asking such questions as *Who is "we"?* and *What don't we want?* are examples of how W³ is used as a heuristic (see Frame 6). Each of the three diagnostic questions is a *leading question* – these questions are easily remembered as well as used to suggest other, *following questions* germane to the three leading questions. When leading questions cannot be easily answered, following questions tend to emerge. By attending to the following questions, you can generate interesting alternative answers to the leading questions.

WHAT DO THEY WANT? Before you can assess their wants, you need to determine who they are. "They" are the various stakeholders – those individuals, groups, and institutions – that have a stake in the actions you take. The number and divergent interests of the various stakeholders can make their assessment problematic. By determining who the relevant "theys" are and what they want, you are identifying possible barriers or constraints with which you may have to contend.

Stakeholder information can be collected by asking the various parties questions about their wants, not just once, but periodically throughout each year. Obtaining such information does not obligate you to satisfy the wants of these stakeholders, rather it identifies areas where there could be mutual benefit and areas that might be best avoided.

As suggested by the overlapping circles shown in Figure 1, the easiest ideas to implement are those ideas that are able to satisfy your wants and the wants of critical stakeholders. The greater the overlap (i.e., the greater the consistency of the goals of effected parties), the greater is your likely success in implementing your ideas. To the extent that some of your goals are not consistent with the goals or constraints imposed by others (i.e., the two circles are not concentric), your efforts to attain those "inconsistent" goals are likely to be stalled, compromised, or made ineffective by people in those environments which have a stake in the issues being addressed.

WHAT CAN WE DO? Developing an understanding of your strengths and capabilities is an idea that is central to any influence process. Organizations and individuals perform more effectively when they are predominantly using established capabilities. This does not imply that new strengths should not be developed; rather, the development of new capabilities should consume a relatively small amount of energy so as not to distract you from leveraging existing strengths. The cost of developing new strengths is high relative to the cost of using a developed strength to achieve growth and development objectives.

If the three W^3 circles are concentric, there is little need to target or focus your energies on accomplishing some goals because all parties can be satisfied. All of your wants are compatible with others' wants and your capabilities. Over time, everything can be accomplished.

As this is rarely the situation, it is important to be able to identify the area of probable overlap. This area is often described as a target market – the market of stakeholders, including customers, that are most likely to want what you want, and can offer. The issues that do make your agenda are a small number of those that could have. Our studies found that people who are able to keep issues moving – often by diagnosing where the suggested solutions do not satisfy all three W^3 questions and then finding solutions that are in the sweet spot – are viewed as more influential and powerful by their associates.

While the W^3 model stimulates thinking around many different wants, constituencies, and capabilities, there will always be a limited set of ideas that simultaneously satisfy the three diagnostic questions. Many of these ideas will not be immediately apparent. This could be graphically presented by the three circles having no area in common. Creativity is often required, particularly in the ways in which you define and interpret issues, to shift the analysis of the situation in ways that lead to some useful "overlaps." This might be done by expanding your wants (making the "What do you want?" circle bigger). Or, it might be done be expanding your capacity or capabilities (making the "What can you do?" circle bigger). Or, it might involve identifying some additional stakeholder wants that were not previously considered (making the "What do they want?" circle bigger). Finally, it may involve redefining the situation such that the various stakeholders view the situation differently, thereby finding some areas of overlap or agreement. This would be like moving the circles closer together.

Not using the W-cubed model can lead to undesirable consequences as Joel found out the hard way. He was a teenager living on an Air Force base. His sister had just received a horse for her sixteenth birthday. He had seen enough westerns to believe he could easily ride this small-looking horse bareback. He knew what he wanted, but failed to consider what the horse might want. He mounted the horse bareback and started to ride towards the horse's favorite trail. The ride went well for about two seconds. Joel thought he could control the horse by using just the reins. He soon discovered that the horse wanted something different – to go back to the paddock. He also discovered that he could not control the horse while riding bareback once the horse embarked on its own agenda.

Things went from bad to worse. Joel managed to turn the horse straight while he was bouncing around on top. Then, at the top of one bounce, the horse turned left. When Joel came down, there was no longer any horse there to land on. He hit the ground hard, and the horse took off for the paddock, which was a quarter mile away – straight across the newly-planted officers' golf course. By not getting at the center of W-cubed, there was hell to pay. Joel ended up grounded, first literally, then figuratively for the next two months by his parents.

How we reach some overlap of **What we want, What they want,** *and* **What we can do,** *is up to each of us. Seeking such overlap is an ongoing challenge.*

---

1. When did you last reach the sweet spot? What was the issue?

2. Was reaching the sweet spot a FLOW experience (as discussed in Frame 2)? Did it involve a convoluted process (as discussed in Frame 17)?

3. Identify an important unresolved issue. What is preventing a sweet spot solution?

4. Reflect on the above mentioned issue. Is life repeating itself (i.e., are you regularly being blocked for similar reasons)?

21 Get Off the Line to Avoid the Think-Act Dilemma

SOMETIMES the world seems divided into two camps; the thinkers and the doers. The thinkers like to ponder a problem and consider its complexities. Before they take action, they want to be comfortable that they are taking the best action possible at that particular time. Doers prefer to take action and experience the outcomes. Why analyze the situation to death? By the time the analysis is done, the situation will be different and the opportunity will have past.

At one time or another most of us have found ourselves in both camps. Our thinking co-campers yell "look before you leap" while the doing co-campers holler "one who hesitates is lost." The line positions in businesses seem full of the doer campers; staff and corporate headquarter positions seem full of the thinker campers. This results in a tension between the two camps that can lead to frustration, conflict, aggression, and/or withdrawal behavior.

The think-more versus act-now tension creates a dilemma. Should we analyze more and potentially miss the opportunity, or should we act now and potentially make a poor quality decision. The think-act dilemma is due to the relationship between the complexity of the issues we face and our mind's ability (and willingness) to make quick decisions. As illustrated in Figure 2, issues vary in their complexity, and people vary in their ability to make quick decisions. Most of us behave in a manner that is reflected by the diagonal line shown in the figure. When dealing with issues high in complexity, we have a limited ability to make quick decisions. When dealing with issues low in complexity, we have substantial ability to make quick decisions.

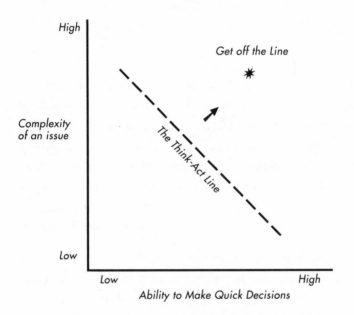

Figure 2. The Think-Act Line

If the people involved in an issue's resolution placed themselves at the same point on the line for an issue, there would be little tension among them. Frequently this is not what occurs in organizations. Those that tend to reside in the thinkers' camp locate themselves higher up on the diagonal line; those residing in the doers' camp locate themselves lower on the diagonal. Because of this relationship, thinkers and doers are often at odds when they could be allies. Doers attack thinkers as purveyors of analysis paralysis. Thinkers counterattack the doers as short-sighted pioneers of the quick fix.

Both positions are initially justified – and equally flawed. The more we understand the complexity of an issue, the less we are able to take decisive actions. One consequence of this relationship is that doers who have the responsibility to take quick action often inappropriately turn a complex issue into a black-white, right-wrong mindset that leads them to make snap judgments. In a doers' camp, indecisiveness is a worse sin than an ineffective decision.

In the thinkers' camp, people make their living finding more and more relevant perspectives from which to view a problem. They learn that every issue has many sides, and no one side has the corner on truth. The price for such under-standing is often an inability to act. A classic story involving President Truman reflects this dilemma:

> Truman frequently asked his chief economic advisor what he should do on various economic policy ques-tions. Each time he asked for advice the economist would say: "Well, on the one hand, if you did this, the consequences would be.... But, on the other hand if you did that, the consequences would be...." At one point President Truman became so exasperated that he shouted, "Damn it, what this country needs is a good one-armed economist!" Times have not changed.

Much of the role of educational institutions – through their emphasis on reading, coursework, and discussion – is to help doers understand the complexity of the issues they will face. The effect of such education may be of little importance until the dilemma between complexity and decisiveness is addressed. *Doers simply cannot afford to see the complexity* of the issues they confront because doing so will slow down their ability to act. If the people involved in the 1.1 million entrepreneurial ventures launched each year in America knew all of the complexities of starting a business, most would not do it.

The world needs both thinkers and doers as key decision makers. If there is an answer to the thinking-doing dilemma it lies in getting off the line altogether. When we stay on the line, we trade off action for complexity or vice versa. Either trade off is a poor one in times of rapid change. If we get off the line, preferably to the right, we will be finding ways to take action while considering the many complexities associated with the issues we confront.

An example came unexpectedly to Joel as he was going into a critical job interview with the Deputy Chairman of the Coopers & Lybrand (C & L) accounting firm. He had arrived in the New York headquarters of C & L from his current job with a different company in Philadelphia. The receptionist took his name then left.

Joel was shocked to find his Philadelphia boss and secretary also waiting in C & L's New York reception area. As he went over to greet his boss and ask what was up, his secretary slipped onto Joel's hands a pair of what seemed like plastic handcuffs. His boss said that this was a symbolic gesture to communicate how much they wanted him to stay with the firm in Philadelphia.

In Joel's words, "At first I was pleased that they went to so much trouble to communicate their interest. Then I noticed the handcuffs were real, and they were not moving to take them off. My boss said that if I was any good, I should be able to handle this adversity. He and my secretary began to leave, said good luck, and took the key with them down the elevator.

"At this moment, the Deputy Chairman's secretary was coming down the hall to get me for the interview. I had but a few seconds to decide what to do. The only options seemed to be to run and make another appointment or to stay and look ridiculous. Sizing up the situation and many of its possible implications, I decided to stay and see it as a challenge. I presented myself with chagrin in such a way the Deputy Chairman laughed. The entire interview was conducted while I was in handcuffs. I think the Deputy Chairman admired how I handled the situation, and I did get the job offer – whew!"

Joel was able to "get off the line." We view getting off the line as developing judgment. Quick fix doers confuse decisiveness with judgment. Procrastinating thinkers confuse analysis with judgment. Doing is not judgment. Analysis is not judgment. Judgment is an integration of analysis and action that permits decisiveness with respect to complex issues. Judgment is perhaps one of the world's most precious skills. It is developed through analysis, action, reflection, and learning. Judgment is that rare off-the-line ability to understand the complexities of an issue and still make a definitive decision when action is needed.

***Good judgment does not come from
either thorough analysis or
decisiveness alone.***

---

1. *Have you ever solved a complex problem
   quickly? How did you do it? What was your
   process? Was your solution successful? Why or
   why not?*

2. *Are others accusing you of delaying a decision
   on some simple issues? Maybe you intuitively
   know that these issues are more complex than
   they appear? How can you resolve this think-act
   dilemma?*

3. *Where do you generally find yourself on the
   Think-Act Line? How do your past experiences
   support this position on the line?*

4. *Where would your mentor place you on the line?
   Your spouse or partner? Your direct reports?
   Your manager? What does this pattern suggest?*

22 Be Both Strategic and Analytic: These Types of Thought Need Each Other

"THINK STRATEGICALLY" – the battle cry of the 1990's. What does it mean to think strategically? Just because everyone is asking for it, does not mean that they know what they are asking for, nor will they necessarily know when they do it.

As we watch managers attempt to think strategically, we see some very different things. Most commonly, thinking strategically means to consider the long term – "What are the implications of our actions today for next year, two years from now, or even five years?" Some managers use the term "thinking strategically" to mean thinking about the relationship of what they are doing relative to the big picture – "What are the implications of our actions in this part of the business today for the enterprise, industry, economy, and/or society as a whole?"

Both of these views of strategic thinking capture some aspects of what it has come to mean. There is a temporal aspect of strategic thinking: Integrating today with tomorrow. Satisfying today's needs in ways that progress towards tomorrow's needs. There is also a spatial aspect of strategic thinking: Integrating the parts with the whole. Operating a part for the best interest of the whole. Figure 3 identifies these two aspects of thinking strategically in a two-by-two grid.

The holistic thinkers that focus on today are often good operating leaders. The temporal thinkers that focus on linking today with the future are good long-term problem solvers. Those who are able to think both spatially and temporally are the best visionary leaders. Their counterparts, the short-term fire-fighters, focus on functional optimization. For example, an executive who secures the launch of a great new product at the expense of production quality or service delivery. This type of thinking is generally more analytical than it is strategic

Spatial Strategic Thinkers	Temporal Strategic Thinkers	
	TODAY	THE FUTURE
WHOLE	Big Picture "Operating Leaders"	Big Movie "Visionary Leaders"
PART	Short-Term "Fire Fighters"	Long-Term "Problem Solvers"

Figure 3. Aspects of Strategic Thinking

We were discussing the idea of strategic thinking with a group of brand managers from Philip Morris – people who have tremendous senior management pressure for short-term results while being expected to guide their brands into the future both temporally and spatially. They generated the ideas shown in Figure 4 for strategic thinking, in contrast to analytic thinking, from a middle management perspective.

Strategic thinking is more...	*Analytical thinking is more...*
• future-oriented	• present-oriented
• broad in perspective & scope	• detailed & focused
• opportunity-oriented	• directed at problem-solving
• divergent	• convergent
• a process and flow	• task- or activity-oriented
• directional	• decisional
• right brain	• left brain
• analogies and comparisons	• discrete and logical

*Figure 4. Comparison of Strategic Thinking
and Analytical Thinking*

As you might expect, most of the brand managers thought that they were doing strategic thinking most of the time on their jobs. Their bosses, in contrast, thought that they were good analytic thinkers, and that they needed to develop the ability to think strategically. Given this feedback from their managers, we decided to discuss how someone else would know when you were thinking strategically. What does strategic thinking *look* like? *Sound* like? What are the aspects of strategic thinking that others can observe?

This discussion started much more slowly than the previous one. But with some patience and reflective thought, the group suggested the following:

Strategic thinking looks, sounds, and feels like...	Analytical thinking looks, sounds, and feels like...
• many iterations	• linear, deterministic
• approximations, reasonable guesses	• forecasts and predictions
• "What if..." questions	• "This is..." statements
• questioning tone	• declarative tone
• ideas stimulate more ideas	• ideas get evaluated and accepted/rejected
• broad issues may remain unresolved	• closure is sought & often obtained
• future possibilities are envisioned	• uncertainty/ambiguity avoided
• conflict is accepted	• conflict is avoided
• few winners or losers emerge	• winners and losers are apparent
• risks are explored	• risks are reduced or avoided
• use of emerging, dynamic models	• use of known, accepted models
• many graphics and visuals	• mostly numbers and words
• being anxious and uncertain	• systematic hard work
• never ending	• resolved
• being uncomfortable	• comfort through logic and use of accepted models
• messy, ill-structured, often hard to follow	• organized, structured, fairly easy to follow conversation flow

Figure 5. The "Sense" of Strategic and Analytical Thinking

Having made these observations, the group was more understanding of why their bosses might not think that they were doing as much strategic thinking as they thought they were. The "face" they put on for senior management was an analytic face; composed, in control, lots of numbers, little uncertainty to predictions, and so on. This is what they thought senior management wanted. Certainly this is what they were taught to do in business school, and what was generally successful in the past.

What they often experienced during their deliberations and discussions with peers and subordinates prior to presentations to senior management was more like the left side above: lots of iterations, lots of questions, lots of debate, many unresolved issues, a fair amount of conflict, little closure, and some discomfort with the process.

One manager commented that he felt that he had to present himself as an analytic thinker, as this was the kind of thinking that senior management really wanted. "If I gave a presentation on my brand that raised questions without providing recommendations, or generated debate and conflict rather than providing direction and answers, I'd be replaced in a week." At first everyone agreed with him – senior management wanted analytic thinking; strategic thinking was a luxury. Then it was suggested that senior management really needed both types of thinking depending on the nature of the issue at hand. This comment led us to a discussion of finding out what others want, and when they might want it. The W-cubed model presented in Frame 20 and the spirit of diagnosis being discovery (Frame 16) became the focus of the subsequent conversation.

**Becoming a visionary leader requires
sharing *the big picture (spatial)* over
time *(temporal)* of the organization
with all of its members.**

---

1. Do you have a preference for one or the other type of thinking? Does your organization? Your manager? Under what conditions, or for what kinds of issues, is this preference most noticeable?

2. How would you categorize your colleagues along the strategic thinking and analytic thinking dimensions. From whom can you learn?

3. How can they contribute to your strengths in this regard?

4. How adept are you at thinking strategically? Where are your blind spots? What are the sources of discomfort or insecurity?

5. In what ways can knowing the unit's vision help you to fight fires?

23 Rules Are Tools (Not to Be Placed in the Hands of Fools)

RULES are created to restrict thought and behavior. They are intended to replace judgment with a "right" answer. In Boston, there is a law forbidding the use of tomatoes in New England clam chowder. Some rules are "hard," other rules are "soft." We suspect that the *no tomatoes* rule is a soft rule.

Following rules may be essential for resolving routine issues and ensuring the smooth running of some aspects of society or an organization. Alternatively, rules may exist long after the situation that they were introduced to control has changed. In such situations, rules inhibit behaviors that could be productive. We wonder if this is why many people get pleasure by doing things that others say they should not do.

Observing the residents of New York City walk the streets of Manhattan is an interesting example of soft rules and how people use rules as tools. New York has a no-jaywalking law. On rare occasions it is enforced. Some pedestrians in New York consciously chose to jaywalk to flaunt the rule. Most ignore the law because it no longer fits the environment. The operational unofficial rule is "don't obstruct traffic." A personal framework behind the unofficial rule might be "don't get hit by a vehicle."

For the first-time visitor to New York the softness of the jaywalking rule may appear to create chaos; yet more people move from one place to another efficiently in New York than in any other city – with a pedestrian accident rate for midtown Manhattan that is not significantly different than other major cities that do enforce their jaywalking laws.

Now contrast this with the rule that "the pedestrian always has the right-of-way" which is actively enacted by pedestrians in California. Many people in California respond to the this rule by freely walking across any street, any time, with barely a glance in either direction. The right-of-way rule exists throughout the United States, but it is tempered in places like New York City by an unofficial rule to "keep both pedestrian and auto traffic moving." Can you imagine the challenge for New York City cabbies in Los Angeles? They expect to be able to keep moving, while the pedestrians are righteous about having the right-of-way.

Rules are best viewed as guidelines that need to be considered in context. We all know that a red light means that we must stop. Yet, as a Brazilian friend, Moises Swirski, once told Steve as they were driving along Copacobana Beach, "some lights are more red than others," and as an after thought, he said, "some are pink." The red light rule was hard during the day when there was a lot of pedestrian traffic moving across the road to the beach and back to their cars; the red light rule was soft at night when few people were using the beach. Knowing when a red light is a symbol of a hard or soft rule is critical to driving in Rio de Janeiro.

Rules provide us with an opportunity to learn from the knowledge and experience of those who created the rule. Acting against a rule is a personal experiment. We deviate from a rule by trying something different with an expectation of what could go well and what could go wrong. The guidance provided by the rule may be valuable and thereby serve to direct our behavior in a manner that is safer or more effective – if so, we have learned something. Alternatively, a rule followed without thought is not a learning experience – it is obedience. Is not the role of a leader to make sensible exceptions to general rules? When and the extent to which we deviate from a rule must be actively considered. Rebelliously breaking rules is no better that blindly following them.

As David Olgivy, author and advertising executive, has said, "Rules are for the obedience of fools and the guidance of wise men."

---

1. Have you broken an "official rule" recently in order to do what was in the broader best interest of the organization? What was the rule?

2. Share this "infraction" with significant others so that they might also develop their sensitivity to soft versus hard rules.

3. What can you do to teach your direct reports (or children, partner) about the difference between soft and hard rules?

4. How is this insight distinct from Frame 18: "Don't Ask the Question if You Can't Live with the Answer?"

24 Raisins Soaked in Water Do Not Become Grapes

I F YOU want grapes, it is best to buy or select them, or to start with something that has a natural tendency to yield grapes – grape vines or grape seeds perhaps. Farmers and vineyard owners know this for it is a critical factor in their business. People in business also know it, but they sometimes act as if they do not.

When someone does not have the ability to perform a task, function, or activity, training is generally believed to be a good solution. Training *only* works when the trainee is motivated to learn and has some potential to be able to perform the task. It may help if the training is designed and implemented effectively. But, focusing on the training content, design, and implementation – which is something those in the training profession do quite well – misses the point. Providing training or other developmental experiences for people who lack the potential or motivation is like soaking raisins to yield grapes. You end up with fat, juicy raisins.

A second point implied by the title is that some processes are not reversible. Cooks and chemists know this, as do you. The implication of recognizing irreversible processes and events is to "dry only as many grapes as you want raisins." Forecast your needs, then act accordingly as there are some things that cannot be undone.

It is often easier to choose, than it is to change.

---

1. Which of your aptitudes are seedlings to be nourished into grapes?

2. What are your limitations (your raisins) that will never yield grapes?

3. Among your associates, might you be trying to turn some raisins into grapes? When should training cease to be the answer to address development? How is your staffing and placement of people leveraging their strengths?

25 "Heathkits™" Are More Valuable Than Solutions

A "HEATHKIT" is a box of parts with a set of instructions on how to build something ourselves. There are Heathkits to build a radio, television, computer, and dozens of other things. Radio Shack sells its own version of Heathkits under its own label.

Heathkits are different from all of those things that we buy that come with a warning, "Some Assembly Required." The "Some Assembly Required" items have not been assembled because it would greatly increase the cost of shipping the item (due to its greater bulk), and/or it would increase the cost of the product (due to the manufacturers' costs of assembly).

Heathkits are not preassembled because then they would not be Heathkits. If we want a radio already assembled, we should buy one. We probably can purchase it for less than the cost of a Heathkit radio. The purpose of a Heathkit is for its user to learn something about what it is that they are constructing. By assembling a radio, one is expected to read about the various parts, find them in a box, and then wire them correctly. Users are learning something about how a radio works. They may also learn something about electronics more generally, as well as their ability to construct something from complex parts which do not look at all like one would expect them to based on their name or function.

When someone asks us for advice in an area where we have reasonable expertise, it is worth pausing before answering to decide whether we should provide a Heathkit or a solution. From our vantage point, we could easily suggest a solution. They ask for something that can provide news summaries, so we give them a radio. From their perspective, a solution from us will be easier and quicker than dealing with a Heathkit.

More often than not, when asked for advice, we provide a solution. We may couch the solution in language that encourages the asker to think about it a bit, or we may provide some possible solutions that must be compared before a decision is made. Rarely do we provide a Heathkit.

If the objective of asking a question is to obtain an answer, the solutional approach works fine. If the objective of asking a question is to learn, then we need to be providing more Heathkits, and fewer solutions. The Peace Corps tries to provide developing nations with Heathkits; the Red Cross focuses more on solutions. Job Training Programs are trying to provide people with Heathkits. Welfare programs focus on solutions.

The problem with Heathkits is that they take time to design and build, and they take time for the user to construct. Do you give someone who wants news updates a Heathkit radio, or Heathkit television? Both will solve her problem. Both are solutions. In order to be able to determine which Heathkit is most appropriate, we need to better understand the problem that the individual is trying to solve – now, as well as over time.

Since we rarely have enough time to do all that we want to do, we tend to skip the Heathkits and go right to the solutions. Everyone seems satisfied with this approach in the short run. And as the economist Keynes said, "In the long run we are all dead." But knowing the final outcome does not mean that the process of getting there should or will be the same for all.

The Heathkit versus solution question comes up often – yet we must be on the lookout for it. A friend asked us how to translate some files from a DOS-based software system to a Macintosh system. Steve was in a hurry, so he rattled off a few instructions. Our friend went back to her Mac to conduct the translation. Steve treated her inquiry as a problem needing a solution, not a person needing a Heathkit. The next time Steve was asked for similar help, he though about it more carefully. He took the Heathkit approach – providing our friend with the pieces, instructions, and the logic behind the activity. She is now answering file translation questions for others, rather than asking us.

---

*Our recipe for providing solicited
advice to others: one Heathkit for
every two solutions; allow Heathkits
to bake twice as long as solutions
in a slow oven.*

---

1. When have you helped others to learn how to do
   something for themselves versus doing it or
   giving them the answer?

2. Are you using the management skill of delega-
   tion with your willing and able direct reports as
   a Heathkit? Frequently enough? What would
   your direct reports say?

3. Are you expecting those who build Heathkits to
   get it right the first time, almost every time?
   What does your answer suggest about your view
   of mistakes?

26 Identify and Observe the Naturals – But Don't Listen to Them

I N almost every field there are people who exhibit what appears to be a natural skill – the baseball player who makes an effortless catch, the singer who bellows out a song that makes your skin tingle, and the journalist that writes an inspiring article. Even within your everyday life, you continually meet and interact with people who seem to exhibit a natural talent: the peer who always can get her ideas listened to by the boss, the child who can recite the top 10 MTV hits (but can't remember how to spell 20 words for a spelling test), and the neighbor that makes every meal a delicious feast (while you still struggle with getting the roast or fish fillet done right). As we observe these people we may become a bit envious. At some point, we make a resolution to improve ourselves in a way that we value.

Having made the decision to improve some area of our lives, we often look for expert advice. Sometimes this takes the form of reading a book about the desired skill. Other times we seek out experts – people who already have the desired ability – and ask for instruction. Or, we find a course or lecture on the topic that gets us both reading and discussing the skill with others. As obviously appropriate as these choices might seem, they are not likely to be very helpful to us in actually acquiring the skill. These methods can provide us with a knowledge base and a conceptual understanding, but they are not likely to lead us to exhibit the skill that we observed occurring so naturally in others.

Most behavioral skills are the result of an intuitive integration of a number of factors. Books can help us to isolate the factors involved, but the real challenge goes beyond understanding; the real challenge is to integrate these factors into our existing capabilities. This is why we are able to recognize many good tips as we read books and articles, but then find that we rarely incorporate these tips into our subsequent actions. There was nothing wrong with the tips or our intentions. Relatively little action occurred because we had not yet determined how the ideas could be integrated into our actions. Our first attempt at this integration probably led us to do some things that we hoped would look like the sought after skill. Of course, our behaviors did not look like those of the naturals. And we know the standard advice: practice, practice, practice. But how do we know that we are practicing the right things?

So we seek out and talk to someone who already has integrated the behaviors into their own skill set. They will be able to tell or show us how to do it. This may not be as fruitful as it first seems. To people who already have a skill, it seems like common sense. We rarely examine the areas of ourselves that we consider common sense. What is common sense to the naturals is uncommon sense for the rest of us. Ask your Aunt Rose or Grandmother how to make one of her famous recipes. The answers we seem to get are to start with the right ingredients, then prepare the dish by adding a bit of this, some of that, mix thoroughly, cook until done, and so on. Somehow, our home made oatmeal bread doesn't taste like Grandma's. We thought we added all the ingredients, kneaded it until firm, and baked it just right.

Talking to naturals about their skills frequently results in non-specific comments such as, "Well, you know, you just gotta focus on what you are doing, and try harder." The problem is that we do not yet know what we are doing – focusing harder on what we don't know is a tough thing to do. When we press for more specific information little is forthcoming, or worse – we get explanations that do not really account for the skill (but we do not know this yet!). This is because behavioral skill in the naturals is often the result of experiences in which the learning process was not entirely conscious. When naturals are pressed to explain themselves they develop answers that may or may not fit the actual reasons for the skill exhibited.

As a consequence, we are typically better off if we observe the behavior of the naturals that we admire, rather than listening to their explanations. Following the directions of naturals may slow our skill development down or prevent us from developing an intuitive integration of the key success factors – given our current level of skill development. It was only after "helping" Grandma make oatmeal bread every Sunday for a year that we internalized what she was saying and doing. I did this by watching, touching, and smelling. In the case of oatmeal bread, it was the touch and smell that I believe made the difference in my skill development. Neither of these senses would have been activated by reading a recipe or listening to Grandma.

> *Beware of advice from naturals; they*
> *frequently are not conscious of what*
> *they are really doing to be effective.*

1. Do you know people who are very effective at
   what they do who attribute their success to
   cliches? Who are they?

2. In observing the behaviors of naturals, try to
   discern what really counts. What do you think
   are the critical success factors of these naturals?

3. Where or in what activities are you a natural? In
   what ways can others learn from you (e.g., by
   observation, by your coaching, by providing
   them with Heathkits)?

27 How to Learn: Your Style Counts

PEOPLE have preferences for how they learn. Some people learn best through *observation and reflection*. They take in the world around them and incorporate aspects of it into their knowledge base. Others learn from their ability to *analyze and generalize* what they see. They formulate models of how they think things will function. They apply these models to other things that seem similar to the original. Still others learn best from *active experimentation* – trial episodes that they create. They test their ideas in new situations to see if they work. Whether they work or not often adds to their knowledge. A fourth preference for learning is through *concrete experience*. People take actions to see what happens. In so doing, they are able to know something that they did not know before.

These four learning preferences, or learning styles, are equally useful ways to learn. Any one of them alone would bias what one could learn due to its limitations. Some things are not easy to observe, or what is observed is not what is actually occurring. Analysis and generalizations tend to loose some of the character and texture of the specific events on which they are based. It is not feasible to conduct experiments around all of life's phenomena, and some experiments alter the phenomena. And, it is not possible to actually experience many things in life, either due to one's abilities, resources, or other limitations.

We are able to learn more and retain it longer when we are able to employ all four of the learning styles. While there is no required order in which to apply these learning methods, it is possible to construct learning cycles. Some stimulus occurs to attract our attention. It may lead us to have a concern over something or someone, or it may be a problem to which we choose to attend. A learning cycle would be to: observe/reflect, then analyze/generalize, then try/experiment, and finally do it for real.

David Kolb's *Experiential Learning* reports several studies of learning styles of people in different professions to see if the preferences that individuals have for their learning style is related to their career choices. Figure 6 summarizes general trends in learning style preferences. For example, retailing positions are more likely to be occupied by people who favor concrete experience and active experimentation as ways of learning. Scholars and research scientists are more likely to favor observation and reflection along with analysis and generalization.

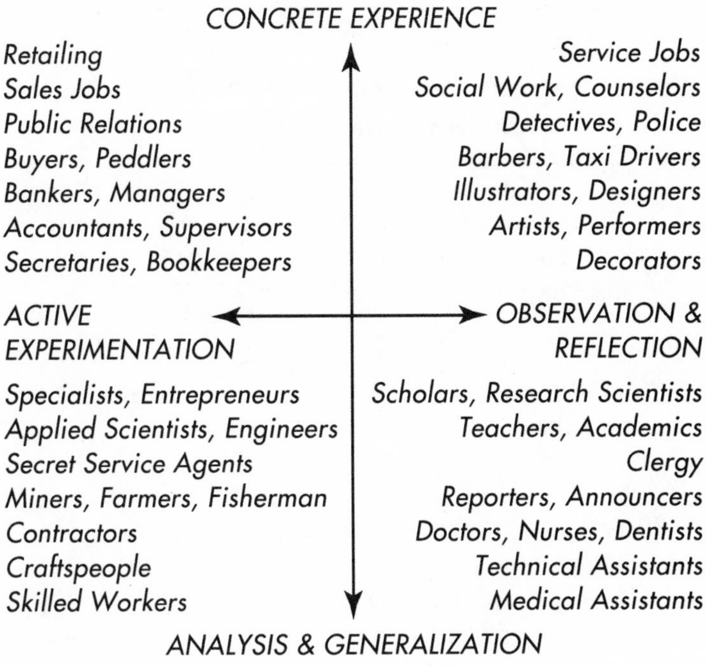

CONCRETE EXPERIENCE

Retailing	Service Jobs
Sales Jobs	Social Work, Counselors
Public Relations	Detectives, Police
Buyers, Peddlers	Barbers, Taxi Drivers
Bankers, Managers	Illustrators, Designers
Accountants, Supervisors	Artists, Performers
Secretaries, Bookkeepers	Decorators

ACTIVE ← → OBSERVATION &
EXPERIMENTATION REFLECTION

Specialists, Entrepreneurs	Scholars, Research Scientists
Applied Scientists, Engineers	Teachers, Academics
Secret Service Agents	Clergy
Miners, Farmers, Fisherman	Reporters, Announcers
Contractors	Doctors, Nurses, Dentists
Craftspeople	Technical Assistants
Skilled Workers	Medical Assistants

ANALYSIS & GENERALIZATION

*Figure 6. Learning the Style Preferences
of Different Career Areas*

To the extent that people's preferences are strong, they may be limiting their opportunities to learn. By developing a capacity to use each of the styles, the depth of knowledge gained on a topic will be greater. Each style brings with it aspects about a phenomenon that were not apparent through the other learning styles.

---

*A master learner is able to integrate
the four learning styles and help
others to do the same.*

---

1. What is your learning style preference? How can you tap into other learning styles so as to improve your mastery of key tasks?

2. Where can you enhance your mastery of a competency by sharing it with others?

3. When you are organizing work groups, teams, or task forces, how can you make sure that all four learning styles are represented?

28 Careers Are Jell-o™

SO YOU think we have gone crazy. The differences between careers and Jell-o are so obvious that discussing
them is ridiculous. Right. So let's explore the similari-
ties. Are careers firm today? Can you pin down a career path?
Are organizations providing a structure (a Jell-o mold) that
changes as we begin to progress in the organization?

Or, do careers get molded and jiggled around to satisfy
the needs of the organization? Has the career ladder that was
articulated when you accepted the position been the ladder
you have been climbing? If the organization had not prom-
ised a career path along a particular ladder, would you be
upset with the progress you have made to date?

Organizations are increasingly unable to define and offer
stable career paths to their employees. It is simply too
difficult to predict their organizational structure, product
lines, key functional areas, and labor needs 10 years ahead.
It has become impossible to predict career movement for the

40 years that most people will work. Career paths are a concept that has utility in stable, predictable environments. If you happen to be in such an industry, then maybe the career paths identified in the past will hold up in the future. Most people are not in such industries – or the industry may be that way today, but will not be by the year 2005. We need to look for a more useful concept for careers than the one that places us along an extension ladder of success. Nailing down a stable, predictable career today is about as easy as nailing Jell-o to the wall.

Are there other ways in which Jell-o and careers are similar? Jell-o comes in different colors and flavors. How about careers? Have you ever thought about the color of your current position? The flavor? Red positions might be a bit hot, blue calm, green growing, yellow envious. What colors do you associate with the various positions in your career? Which flavors? Which where the desirable ones, why?

Can you use your sense of color and flavor to guide your career decisions in the future? Your choice of a red hot career a few years back may need to be updated. Careers that require energy and activity are well-suited to the young. Are they still well-suited for you? Careers that demand extensive wisdom are better suited for people who have invested the time and obtained the experience to develop some wisdom. Remember the Pennsylvania Dutch expression, "Ve get too soon old and too late smart." Maybe your Jell-o has gone flat or become rubbery (it does you know). Or maybe you are ready for a different flavor now that your experiences have cultivated your tastes. You may even be ready to try Jell-o Pops™ or Royal pudding.

---

*Before we become overly concerned
that our career has not progressed as
planned, check the plan. Our work
activities may be closer to the
flavors and colors that we
want than we first thought.*

---

1. Think of your career as a series of activities and projects that you enjoy doing. What are these activities and projects? Why do you enjoy doing them?

2. As you hire people, what notion of "career" are you communicating? If careers are more like Jell-o than ladders to be climbed in your organization, how can you communicate this effectively to recruits?

29 Don't Play the Blame Game – Accept and Learn from Your Mistakes

HAVE you noticed that many people today place the blame on others for their mistakes. They attribute anything bad that happens in their lives to other people or an unfair system. Through this attribution, they often deny or ignore the role they had in the unfortunate event.

A magazine article reported the outrage of a father that his son was arrested in a drug investigation at the son's fraternity house. The father wanted to know why the police raided his son's fraternity and not all the other fraternities. The father's outrage was not that he believed that his son was innocent, or that the son was wrongfully accused. The issue was that his son got caught and many others who probably were committing a similar crime did not.

What ever happened to the following the guidance of George Washington after he felled a cherry tree? If George were around today, he would have scolded his father for not removing the tree from the proximity of where he was playing, or for not keeping him otherwise occupied so that he did not become aware of his hunger and the cherry tree. If George admitted his mistake today, the attorneys would laugh at him.

There is a difference between being a victim, and attributing anything bad that happens to us to other people or faulty systems (e.g., biased police). Victims are casualties. They are people who wrongly suffer a loss. Evading taxes and getting caught is not being a victim. Nor are we a victim when we are caught breaking other rules or laws.

Of course, we all violate some rules some of the time – from speeding to opening a spouse's mail to jaywalking to parking our car near a fire hydrant. Now and then we get caught. This may be bad luck; but, it is not being a victim. To treat this as victimization denies us the learning opportunity and often places demands on other systems as we try to get restitution for our perceived victimization.

Playing the blame game positions us as "victims."

---

1. When was the last time you refused to play "spread the blame" when something you were involved with went wrong? When was the last time you did *play it?* Why?

2. Being seen as a victim communicates to those around you that you are not to be held accountable for your actions. If you want them to be accountable for their actions, how can you help them to avoid the "victim" positioning?

3. Think of an incident in which you were involved that was perceived by significant others as a mistake. How did they respond? Who took responsibility? Who was blamed?

4. What do you do when people at work go into the "victim" mode? Do you help them to see how they are empowered and point out areas where they could take more responsibility?

30 Accommodate Diversity Through Flexible Simplicity

DIVERSITY can be a stimulating and interesting thing. Many say that diversity is what has made America a great country to live in. Diverse backgrounds, perspectives, and beliefs merging into one society gives the nation a creativity potential and zest that is unsurpassed by any other country. Yet, with all of the words about how diversity is a benefit, we are often at a loss as to how to accommodate it successfully.

A phrase, often used by observers of the Clarence Thomas hearings during the fall of 1991, captures the challenge of accommodating diversity for the next decade: "You just don't get it." Men did not get the significance of sexual harassment to women; women did not get how vulnerable men felt to be subject to conviction by accusation; Whites did not get the nature of the degrading sex-role some Black men have perpetuated towards Black women; Black women did not get the embarrassment felt by Black men by having their masculinity displayed to the public, and so on. The implication of "You just don't get it" is that the only way to understand someone else's point of view and emotions is to be one of them. Men can never understand women's emotions because they are not women. Whites can never understand the impact of racism and discrimination on others because they are not Native American, Hispanic, African American, or Asian.

If we take the idea of "You just don't get it" to its logical endpoint, we would conclude that diversity is the cause of all misunderstandings, conflicts, and strife. If we could eliminate the diversity, then life would be a more pleasant experience. If only everyone was the same. It only takes a few moments reflection on this possibility to discard it entirely. Diversity is important; we need to learn how to both enjoy it and accommodate it when it becomes threatening.

Given how valuable diversity can be, why is it often so hard to accommodate it – particularly in organizations? Think of the last mini-conflict that you experienced in an organization or social situation. Maybe it was at work, or in a retail store, or at the bank, or as a driver dealing with other drivers. Why did the mini-conflict occur? There were your actions and points of view, and there were the other parties' actions and points of view. You probably felt what you were doing was either right, or at least acceptable in the situation. And, so did they. If the conflict escalated, words were exchanged and stronger emotions were felt than on similar occasions without such conflict. Or, maybe you decided to accommodate the situation – you said, "So what's the difference, have it your way."

In practice, accommodating diversity means tolerating differences. Yet organizations, as social systems, tend to create and support sameness. Organizations create rules, roles, and procedures to reduce the diversity of behaviors exhibited within their boundaries. Organizations often select people for membership that already conform to their system, or who it is believed will be able to adjust to the system. The economies of scale that allow large organizations to prosper are often based on finding the "one best way" to make things, or the "one size fits all" way to sell them. Mass production, product consistency, and work efficiency are much easier when there is little diversity. Henry Ford's, "Any color you want as long as it is black" dictum is an example. In such environments differences are seen as problems that have to be handled, they are deviations from the norm and sources of conflict.

If we are to make progress in taking advantage of diversity, we have to find ways of accommodating differences efficiently. One way to think about accommodating diversity is through a flexible simplicity approach. Flexible in that most people can have it their way. Simple in that it is easy to accommodate the diverse preferences. *Flexible simplicity requires you to find an underlying core element or value that is common to the diverse points of view.* A few examples may illustrate the flexible simplicity approach.

Burger King approached the differences in customer preferences for toppings on their hamburgers by letting the customer put their own toppings on. Other fast food hamburger restaurants make people who want a non-standard hamburger wait for it, on the side, while they continue serving other customers. Burger King saw the core element as the hamburger and bun; not a fully dressed hamburger.

The modern paint store is another example. There are several hundred different colors of several different types of paint (latex, oil-based, glossy, semi-gloss, flat). If, to implement an "any color and type of paint that you want" offer, the store had to stock quarts and gallons of every combination, the inventory costs would soon drive the owner out of business. Fortunately, the diversity of colors customers need can be met by blending a few primary colors into a white base. By stocking only the primary colors and the different base paints, and having a way to flexibly and precisely combine them, the paint store can handle thousands of unique requests. The simple core is the science of mixing colors; the flexibility is in combining and mixing the paint after it is ordered.

By maintaining an "accommodate diversity" mindset, it is possible to remain open to a broad spectrum of different issues while looking for a simple core to these issues. Doing this often requires creativity to find ways to avoid developing a unique product or program for every distinctive need that arises.

Is there a flexible simplicity solution to the "You just don't get it" concern expressed by many observers of the Clarence Thomas hearings? The simple core for us is human dignity. We do not believe that one has to be female or African American or any particular combination of race, religion, sex, age, and cultural background to accommodate differences as long as human dignity is at the core of the relationships.

Diversity is all around us. We all are different, yet we all have things in common. We can accommodate many differences through flexibility around that common core.

---

1. *Reflect on all of the sources of diversity in your organization. How can you tap into that valuable pool of different strengths so as to benefit the organization and validate the worth and dignity of each individual? List a few names and ideas below.*

2. *Focus on a current conflict in your organization or family – particularly one that is fueled by differences in style or approach. Can you find a simple premise of agreement? Can this area of agreement be used to create greater flexibility among the players so as to resolve the issue?*

31 Being Unreasonable May Be the Most Reasonable Approach

C HARLES HANDY'S book, *The Age of Unreason,* captures what many people have suspected for years, but have been slow to articulate: change has become less predictable and less understandable, and we must do some "upside-down" thinking to deal with it. Change has often occurred in knowable and predictable ways. The growth and widespread use of forecasts and statistical methods has been the rational person's answer to change. Predict it, plan for it, adjust to it. As long as there is no discontinuity, the past can be used to predict the future with some accuracy and reliability. Once discontinuities occur, it is hard to know what information can be used to direct rather than misdirect future activities.

A discontinuity is a break from a trend or past pattern of behavior. Sneaker sales in the 1970's were increasing slowly each year in response to the number of youth in the population. Then a discontinuity occurred: Nike redefined sneakers to be a variety of different athletic shoes and Reebok redefined them as fashion foot ware. The traditional tennis shoe style sneaker sales fell, and the new style "sneaker" sales tripled within two years. Electric memory typewriter sales skyrocketed as computerization of the office equipment market took hold, then fell off as sharply as it had risen when personal computers began to replace typewriters and word processors. Both of these discontinuities forced unpredicted, radical change on the manufacturers of the older line of products. New lines of business were formed, existing lines that were slow to change floundered.

Handy suggests that being unreasonable is one way to accommodate radical, discontinuous change. Yet most of us suffer from the unreasonable expectation that all things should be reasonable; to be unreasonable is unreasonable.

Being unreasonable means suggesting and doing things that are not necessarily linearly related to the current situation. If we only consider the next logical step from where we are now, we will have trouble keeping up. We need to use the discontinuous changes that we experience to stimulate our upside-down thinking. If A leads to B, then lets consider whether or not it can make sense for B to lead to A. If more is better, then let's consider whether or not less is more. Less weight and volume are more desired and more expensive when it comes to laptop and notebook computers. Upside-down thinking encourages us to consider the unlikely. It stimulates our creative potential.

---

*When there is a break from
expectations or past trends, the
unreasonable explanation may be
the most useful one.*

---

1. What unreasonable explanations have you
   heard recently? What new information would
   make these explanations seem more reasonable?

2. Can you see any connections between being
   unreasonable and being creative?

3. Make a list of five unreasonable questions you
   might ask that would turn people's thinking
   upside-down. Use these to help the organization
   identify viable options for the future.

32 Advanced Technology Is Indistinguishable From Magic

THAT explains it. We no longer have to feel bad for not understanding how all of those technological gadgets work – or how to work them.

If advanced technology is a mix of witchcraft and wizardry, and we have purposely chosen not to become magicians, then we are not obliged to understand advanced technology. We can observe the magic, have it work for us, and enjoy the illusion.

We do not need to feel guilty, angry, or incompetent because we do not understand how to fix the car, video-record a movie, setup a spreadsheet on the computer, or answer our 13-year old's math and science questions. There are magicians around who can do these things. We need to know who they are, ask for a display of their skills, and applaud their performances.

Observing other people's magic is one side of the coin. The other side, to others, is that much of what we do as professionals and knowledge workers is magic. Sometimes we try to explain our magic to others – this is tough going. We overwhelm the newcomer with jargon, details, and complexity that is useful to us, not them. If we are successful in our explanations, the magic becomes no more than a sleight of hand; an illusion that has been discovered. Hence we work hard at advancing our technology so as to make it indistinguishable from magic.

A sales manager of The Principal Financial Group was recently expressing some frustration with a computer system called CCA. He said that CCA would be a great system when they finished tailoring it to the needs of the sales force, but for now, it was an irritant.

I asked what was meant by the initials CCA. He said that he did not know. I asked what software or language was used in CCA. He said he didn't know that either. I asked why CCA was an irritant. He said that it required him to learn various computer commands and reporting protocols that were not easy to remember. CCA was a home office program that was meant to be of benefit to the field agency force. "Someday," the sales manager assured me, "CCA will be of great value to me with all of its capabilities." Maybe that is all the sales manager needed to know.

If the rapid rate of technological change forces this reality upon us, why not accept it as an insight? We cannot keep up with all of the changes taking place, nor is keeping up with them how we want to spend our time. There are too many updates and enhanced versions of last year's technology to master. We may not need to invest the time or energy to learn how to do someone else's latest magic.

We should spend our energy in appreciating others' magic and focus on learning how to use our magic to make progress on our agenda.

---

1. *What technologies seem magical to you? To your spouse, co-workers, or children?*

2. *What do you do that seems magical to others? How can you become a better magician?*

33 Foster Continuous Learning by Embracing Waves of Change

CHANGE has changed, and change is not fair anymore. While we feel this way today, our parents probably felt this way 25 years ago, and our grandparents felt this way 25 years before that. They may still feel that way, or they may have developed a set of coping mechanisms to embrace or buffer themselves from change. No matter how they are handling it, change is still happening at ever increasing rates.

What makes change so uncomfortable is that it is often unpredictable *and* we have to do things differently if we accept the change. Change may not lead to more comfortable behaviors, at least not initially. So, few people really like change – with the exception of wet babies!

We see people respond in one of three ways to the increasing rates of change in the workplace. Some resist.

Some "hang-in-there." Some accept change and embrace its opportunities.

Resisting change is a short-term solution. If the change is driven by forces beyond the actions of one's immediate co-workers, it eventually overtakes all but the best resistors. It is like a wave crushing down on you – frightening, disorienting, and potentially fatal.

Hanging-in-there is the "treading water" approach to change. You hope that you can outlast the storm and that the waves will become more manageable again. Maybe you can keep you head above water indefinitely. But this is extremely stressful and not very productive. We gain little of the benefits of the past or the excitement of the future.

Learning to go with change is like a surfer learning to ride the waves. Surfers learn to read the waves and control their surf board. We need to learn how to read the directions of change and ride our values. This can lead to a dynamic stability that is exhilarating.

To develop this third response to change requires continuous learning, and continuous learning requires the ability to develop insights. We need to develop new connections as change moves the dots of our experience around, and adds new dots in near random locations. By learning to develop insights, we increase our power to use what we already know to enrich our lives. We hope that we have contributed to that outcome.

1. In what ways was this book of value to you?

2. How might you use it in the future?

PREVIEW OF VOLUME II

INSIGHTS need to be integrated into a context of experiences to which you can personally relate. In doing this, insights become lessons or learnings that are useful in enriching your life and those around you. Keep the role of insight in sight as you go about life. When you have a new insight, jot it down to savor it a while longer. Send it to us if you are interested in sharing it with others.

We have begun capturing insights for a future volume. Some tentative titles are:

- Group meetings are essential to group effectiveness, but group meetings are the worst place to make group decisions.

- Paradox is the leaders' arena: Join the circle.

- Creating a shared vision is the most efficient form of control.

- Keep most goals as outcomes, not the reason for which you are working.

- The need for a data compass.

- Don't just do something, stand there: Awaiting crisis.

- Rational thinking is the language, not the behavior of business.

- Set direction, identify a leader, then serve that leader.

- Sometimes you have to bet the farm, but not every day.

- Practical risk taking; two shots and then salute

- You can never walk all your talk; don't expect to.

- Go crazy now and then, or you'll go crazy.
- In the land of the nearsighted, a person with 20/20 vision will appear strange.
- Don't expect headquarters to ever get its act together; few are prepared for life in the land of the bosses.
- Don't balance your life, integrate it.
- Professional play can yield more work than a work orientation.
- Don't compare, excel.
- Living with the power-trust paradox.
- Problem-solving is not decision-making.
- Don't try to manage change, create new stabilities.
- Understanding leverage: Using one stone to tumble a wall.
- Trust is the most efficient way to make money.
- Let power go to your feet, not your head.
- Tapping into the most powerful metaphor; the pinball effect.
- If a problem cannot be solved, it is not a problem.
- Help manipulators to self-destruct.
- Learning is more about letting go than acquiring.
- A penny saved is a lost opportunity.
- If you want the dollars to balance, manage the dimes.
- Single source validity is no validity at all.
- At work, lead with your head and check it with your heart; at home, lead with your heart, and check it with your head.

- Learning from experience, empathy before strategy.

- Men and women come from the same solar system, but different planets.

- Greed and Fear versus Leadership and Excellence.

- Money is worth something: Freedom.

- Use work as a proving ground for character development.

- In facilitating change, the right questions are more powerful than the right answers.

- Avoid top management commitment to your great ideas.

- The X factor: You cannot escape chaos.

- Facilitate a good design, don't try to use facilitation to make up for design flaws.

- Business leaders use command when they don't know how to lead.

- Change is completely different than problem-solving.

- Why we are lousy at group problem-solving?

- Inertia is a living system's safety valve; don't mistake it for resistance.

- Organizational change follows the marketing curve.

- Change is inherently destructive.

- How pay systems rob Peter to pay Paul and destroy teamwork.

- An insight is its own reward.

Join us in our next adventure.

Stephen A. Stumpf

Stephen A. Stumpf is the Director of the Center of Leadership and Professor of Management at the College of Business, The University of Tampa. From 1984 to 1993, he was Professor of Management and Director, Management Simulation Projects Group at the Leonard N. Stern School of Business, New York University.

He is a director and cofounder of the MSP Institute – a research and development organization that serves both the educational and corporate community with new technologies for leadership development.

He received his doctorate in organizational behavior from New York University in 1978. He is the author or c-oauthor of six books on careers and management development and is a regular contributor to the Journal of Management Development, Academy of Management Journal and Journal of Strategic Management.

Dr. Stumpf's management development work includes the design and use of eleven large-scale management simulations, now used by many corporations in their management development work and by universities across the country as educational tools in their business programs. He has consulted with many businesses including Philip Morris, Citicorp/Citibank, Dow Jones, AT&T, Aetna, Smith Barney Shearson, Metropolitan Life, and Northern Telecom.

Steve was a 1986 Fulbright Scholar in Brazil and won the 1990 David L. Bradford Outstanding Educator Award for his contributions to the fields of leadership and organizational behavior.

Joel R. DeLuca

Joel R. DeLuca is a consultant in the management of change. He heads his own consulting business and is currently on the faculty of New York University's Business School. He taught at the Wharton Business School in 1984 and 1985.

He received a doctorate in Organizational Behavior from Yale in 1981. He has published two books and articles in the Human Resources Planning journal, and the Organizational Development Network journal.

From 1981 ro 1989, Dr. DeLuca was head of organizational planning and executive development for the Sun company, and from 1989 to 1993 of human resource planning for Coopers and Lybrand. He has consulted for a variety of public and private organizations. For the last four years he has reviewed research related to strategic change for the Academy of Managment.

As a Captain in the United States Air Force, he worked as a research scientist on solar cell systems for satellites. It was during this work that he made a career shift into the organizational sciences.

Dan Shefelman

Dan Shefelman is a cartoonist and illustrator living in Nw York City. After receiving a B.A. degree in political science from Kenyon College (1984) Shefelman became editorial cartoonist for the Austin American-Statesman and was syndicated internationally. He moved to New York in 1990 to take the position of editorial cartoonist at New York Newsday, where he created a business editorial cartoon, *Funny Money*,which was subsequently syndicated.

His caricatures of celebrities have been featured on the game show, *Rumor Has It*. He was design director for Nickelodeon's animated series, *Doug*.

INDEX